# Literary Analysis

# &

# Essay Writing Guide

by

Colin Shanafelt

Gatsby's Light Publications

Austin, Texas

Published by Gatsby's Light Publications, LLC
Austin, Texas
www.GatsbysLight.com
contact@GatsbysLight.com

First Edition

ISBN 978-0-9829895-3-1

Gatsby's Light Publications

# Literary Analysis Guide

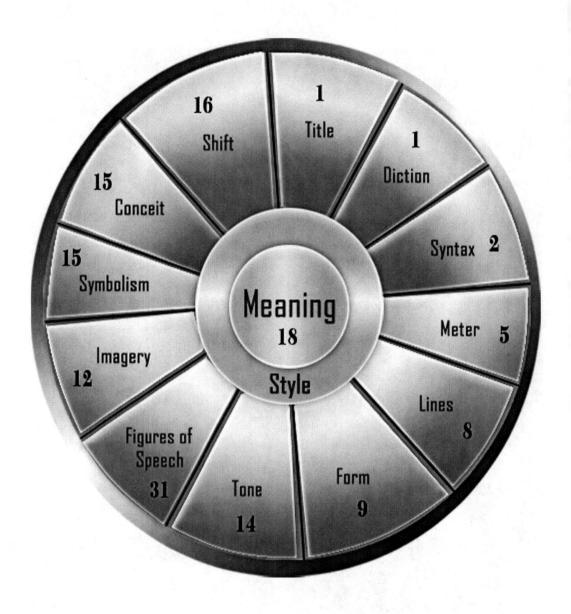

# Poetry

# Prose

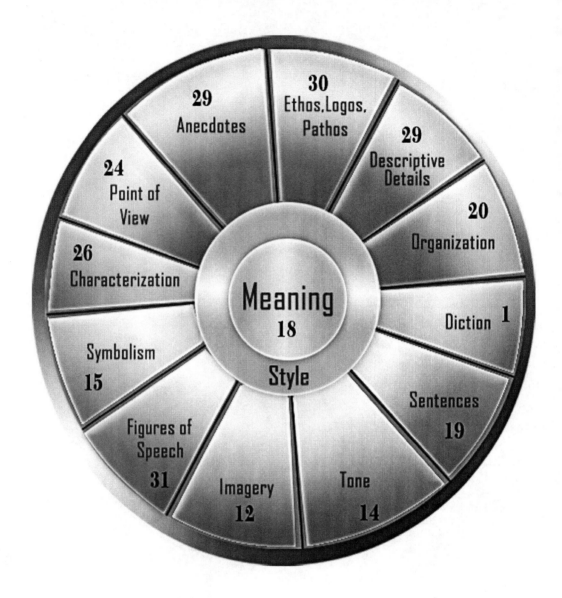

# Rhetoric

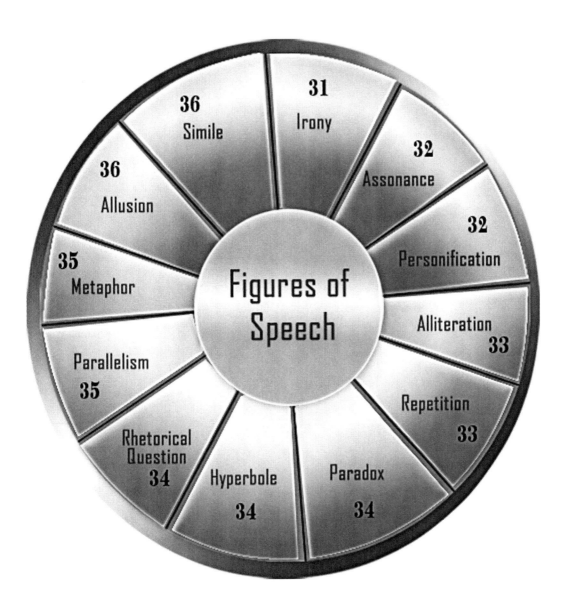

# Figures of Speech

# Title

Usually, the reader's first experience with a literary work is its title. The title of a work can often be the key to gaining a better understanding of its overall meaning. For poetry, read the title before you read the poem, then go back and read the title again after you finish. Some poets like to imbed the meaning of their poems in the title.

### Examples
- "A Valediction: Forbidding Mourning"- John Donne
- *The Sound and the Fury* - William Faulkner
- "Summum Bonum" - Robert Browning
- "Leaves of Grass" - Walt Whitman

### Questions To Ask
- Does the title stand out from the story in any way?
- Is it an odd title? If so, it may hold the key to a different, perhaps better, interpretation.
- Is the title an allusion? If so, to what, and how does that allusion deepen the meaning of the work?
- What makes this word or group of words so important that it warrants being chosen as the title?

# Diction

Diction refers to the type of words an author chooses (i.e. vocabulary). Sometimes, diction can be characterized as high, middle, or low, depending on the degree of sophistication and formality of the words used. Mark Twain is famous for saying, that difference between the right word and the almost right word is the difference between lightning and a lightning bug." Diction has a profound effect on many other elements of literature such as imagery, characterization, and tone. Diction can often be the key to understanding the meaning of a piece.

Analyze diction by first deciding what type or types of words have been used. Then decide how those types of words develop tone, emotion, and/or meaning. Be specific in your discussion of diction by quoting actual words from the text, by describing the character of those words (e.g. highly active and kinetic verbs), and by showing how those words build tone, emotion, or meaning.

## Examples

- *Moby-Dick* contains a chapter titled "The Try-Works" in which Herman Melville uses words like "fierce," "Tartarean," "pagan," "pronged poles," "hissing," "scalding," "snaky flames," "boiling," "scorched," "tawny," "begrimed," "barbaric," "fire," "red hell," and "emblazonings" to evoke feelings and images of hell, evil, horror, and torment.
- In "After great pain, a formal feeling comes" Emily Dickinson uses words like "Tombs," "stiff," "mechanical," "Wooden," "Quarts," "stone," and "lead" to convey a feeling like the heavy, unnatural, and gradual hardening sensation one feels after a great heartbreak.

### Questions To Ask

- What is different about the author's nouns, verbs, adjectives, etc.?
- Find an adjective for the type of words the author generally uses: technical, flowery, colloquial, cerebral, punning, obscure, flashy, polysyllabic, ten-dollar, simple, cliche, etc.
- How do the words that are chosen affect the actual sound of the piece (e.g. through other literary devices such as alliteration, assonance, consonance, etc.)?
- Are the words sharp, hot, heavy, hard, sad, opaque, etc.?

# Syntax

Syntax is word order. More specifically, syntax is the way an author chooses to group words within clauses, phrases, and sentences. To analyze syntax, look for unique word order and decide how that unique language develops meaning in the text.

## Examples

- "Madness in great ones must not unwatch'd go." vs. Great ones who are mad should not go unwatched. - William Shakespeare
- "Love is not love that alters when it alteration finds." vs. Love is not love that alters when it finds alteration. - William Shakespeare
- "I and this mystery here we stand" vs. This mystery and I stand here - Walt Whitman
- "Here I opened wide the door;" vs. I opened the door wide here - Edgar Allan Poe
- "Whose woods these are I think I know" vs. I think I know whose woods these are. - Robert Frost

# Syntax Techniques

## Juxtaposition
A literary device in which two very dissimilar things (i.e. words, ideas, objects, characters, etc.) are compared or contrasted to achieve a new and interesting effect.

## Examples
- "John Donne - Ann Donne - Undone." - John Donne
- "Were vexed to nightmare by a rocking cradle" - William Butler Yeats
- "No light, but rather darkness rather visible" - John Milton
- "Suddenly I saw the cold and rook-delighting Heaven / That seemed as though ice burned and was but the more ice," - William Butler Yeats

## Omission
The intentional omission of words, clauses, or phrases.

## Examples
- "And he to England shall along with you."- William Shakespeare
- "He works his work, I mine. - Alfred, Lord Tennyson
- "So that, forever rudderless, it went upon the seas / Going ridiculous voyages" - Stephen Crane "The Black Riders"

## Parallel Structure (Parallelism)
Using like grammatical structure, diction, and phrasing to correlate successive clauses and phrases, both within and among sentences.

## Examples
- "Ask not what your country can do for you; ask what you can do for your country." - John F. Kennedy
- "The prince's strength is also his weakness; his self-reliance is also isolation." - Machiavelli
- "There is a time in every man's education when he arrives at the conviction that envy is ignorance; that imitation is suicide; that he must take himself for better, for worse, as his portion;" - Ralph Waldo Emerson

## Repetition
Reusing the same words or phrases for rhythmic or rhetorical effect.

## Example
"We must fight! I repeat it, sir, we must fight!" - Patrick Henry

## Polysyndeton

The use of multiple coordinating conjunctions in series to create a sense of rhythm or a tone of excitement and energy.

### Examples

- "[A]s the wind howled on, and the sea leaped, and the ship groaned and dived, and yet steadfastly shot her red hell further and further into the blackness of the sea and the night, and scornfully champed the white bone in her mouth, and viciously spat round her on all sides; then the rushing Pequod, freighted with savages, and laden with fire, and burning a corpse, and plunging into that blackness of darkness, seemed the material counterpart of her monomaniac commander's soul." - Herman Melville - *Moby-Dick*
- I mete and dole / Unequal laws unto a savage race, / That hoard, and sleep, and feed, and know not me." - Alfred, Lord Tennyson

## Anaphora

The repetition of the same word or group of words at the beginning of neighboring clauses.

### Example

"We shall not flag or fail. We shall go on to the end. We shall fight in France, we shall fight on the seas and oceans, we shall fight with growing confidence and growing strength in the air, we shall defend our island, whatever the cost may be, we shall fight on the beaches, we shall fight on the landing grounds, we shall fight in the fields and in the streets, we shall fight in the hills. We shall never surrender." - Winston Churchill

## Epanalepsis

The repetition at the end of a clause of the word that occurred at the beginning of the clause.

### Examples

- "Possessing what we still were unpossessed by, / Possessed by what we now no more possessed." - Robert Frost
- "To each the boulders that have fallen to each." - Robert Frost
- "The king is dead, long live the king. / What is Hecuba to him, or he to Hecuba?" - William Shakespeare

## Questions To Ask

- Does the word order sound like natural human speech, or highly stylized?
- Are there any words that seem to be left out or rearranged?
- Is the word order (syntax) straightforward or unconventionally crafted?
- What effect does the unique word order of the piece have on the overall meaning of the work?

# Meter

The meter of a poem refers to the pattern of stressed and unstressed syllables both in and among its lines. Identify meter by determining the most common type of foot and the number of feet per line (e.g. iambic pentameter = five iambic feet). When analyzing a poem based upon its meter, try to determine how the rhythm of the poem further develops meaning.

**Foot -** One stressed syllable plus the unstressed syllables that seem to go with it:
\ = Stressed Syllable    ~ = Unstressed Syllable

## Types of Feet

| FOOT | NOUN | ADJECTIVE |
|------|------|-----------|
| ~ / | Iamb | Iambic |
| ~ ~ / | Anapest | Anapestic |
| / ~ | Trochee | Trochaic |
| / ~ ~ | Dactyl | Dactylic |
| // | Spondee | Spondaic |

## Types of Meter

| FEET / LINE | PREFIX | METER |
|-------------|--------|-------|
| 1 | Mono | Monometer |
| 2 | Di | Dimeter |
| 3 | Tri | Trimeter |
| 4 | Tetra | Tetrameter |
| 5 | Penta | Pentameter |
| 6 | Hex | Hexameter |
| 7 | Hepta | Heptameter |
| 8 | Oct | Octameter |

**Example**

### Sonnet 129

Th' expense of spirit in a waste of shame
Is lust in action: and till action, lust
Is perjur'd, murd'rous, bloody, full of blame,
Savage, extreme, rude, cruel, not to trust;
Enjoy'd no sooner but despised straight;
Past reason hunted; and, no sooner had,
 Past reason hated, as a swallow'd bait,
On purpose laid to make the taker mad:
Mad in pursuit and in possession so;
Had, having, and in quest to have, extreme;
A bliss in proof, and prov'd, a very woe;
Before, a joy propos'd; behind, a dream.
All this the world well knows; yet none knows well
To shun the heaven that leads men to this hell.

**- William Shakespeare**

## Iambic Pentameter

| ~ | / | ~ | / | ~ | / | ~ | / | ~ | / |
|------|------|------|------|------|------|------|------|------|------|
| Th' ex | pense | of | spir | it | in | a | waste | of | shame |
| ~ | / | ~ | / | ~ | / | ~ | / | ~ | / |
| Is | lust | in | act | ion; | and | till | act | ion, | lust |
| ~ | / | ~ | / | ~ | / | ~ | / | ~ | / |
| Is | pur | jur'd, | murd' | rous, | bloo | dy, | full | of | blame, |

## Examples of Meter

- Iambic pentameter - (Christopher Marl owe, The Tragical History of Doctor Faustus; Edna St. Vincent Millay, Sonnets)
- Dactylic hexameter - (Homer, Iliad; Virgil, Aenead, Ovid - "The Metamorphoses")
- Iambic tetrameter - (Alexander Pope; Andrew Marvell -"To His Coy Mistress")
- Iambic heptameter - (Robert Louis Stevenson)
- Trochaic octameter - (Edgar Allan Poe -"The Raven")
- Anapestic tetrameter - (Lewis Carroll -"The Hunting of the Snark"; Lord Byron, Don Juan)
- Trochaic tetrameter - (many hymns)

## Vocabulary of Poetic Meter

1. Blank Verse - Unrhymed iambic pentameter.
2. Caesura - A natural pause in a line of poetry, indicated by natural rhythm rather than meter.
3. Common Meter - Alternating lines of four beats (iambic tetrameter) and three beats (iambic trimeter). This was Emily Dickinson's chosen meter.
4. Free Verse - Poetry that lacks meter, rhyme, and strict regulation of line length.
5. Prosody - The study of form in poetry (i.e. meter, rhyme, rhythm, and stanzaic structure).
6. Scansion - The analysis of poetic meter using symbols for stressed and unstressed syllables (i.e. to "scan" a poem).
7. Verse - Any literature that is broken into lines and/or employs a regular meter.

## Examples

- Emily Dickinson predominantly wrote in "common meter" (i.e. four-line stanzas alternating between iambic tetrameter and iambic trimeter, a meter used in many nursery rhymes and hymns such as "Amazing Grace"), but most scholars agree that she did so only in order to intentionally break the meter with caesuras and dashes thus reinforcing her belief in non-conformity.
- In "Sonnet 129," Shakespeare uses a contraction to combine the word "the" with the first syllable of the word "expense." In doing so, he forces the reader to read the line (and poem) rapidly, thus reinforcing the sonnet's theme of that man is a lusty, clamorous being who is constantly "Mad in pursuit" of something.

## Questions To Ask

- How does the poet's particular choice of meter affect the rhythm and sound of the poem?
- Does the meter enhance or further develop the meaning of the poem? How?
- Does the meter seem to produce a musical quality?
- Does the meter develop the tone of the piece?

# Lines

The traditional definition of poetry is as follows: "Any written composition that is deliberately separated into lines." Therefore, the line is one of the most powerful tools a poet uses to developing meaning and is the core of poetry itself.

## End-Stopped Line
A line of poetry that comes to a grammatical conclusion at its termination. The full meaning or the line seems complete.

## Example
from **"A Poison Tree"**
I was angry with my friend:
I told my wrath, my wrath did end.
I was angry with my foe:
I told it not, my wrath did grow.
### - William Blake

## Enjambment
A poetic thought or grammatical structure that extends beyond one line. Enjambed lines do not end with grammatical breaks, and their sense is not complete without the following line(s).

## Example
from **"Thanatopsis"**
Yet not to thine eternal resting -place
Shalt thou retire alone, nor couldst thou wish Couch more magnificent. Thou shalt lie down With patriarchs of the infant world, with kings, the powerful of the earth, Th wise, the good, Fair forms, and hoary seers of ages past,
All in one mighty sepulchre. The hills . . .
### - William Cullen Bryant

## Questions To Ask
- Do the line breaks create additional meaning, double meanings, or ambiguity within the poem?
- If the lines are broken in what seems like odd places, why do you think the poet chose those places to break the lines?
- How do the poem's line breaks affect its tone and rhythm?
- Do you think the poet wants you to pause at the end of a line or read straight through?

# Form

Generally, the form of a poem involves its number of stanzas, rhyme scheme, traditional pattern (if any), spacing, refrain, stanzaic breaks, and other such qualities.

**Stanza** - A group of lines set apart from the rest of the poem by empty space.

## Types of Stanzas

| | |
|---|---|
| 2 lines – Couplet | 6 lines – Sestet |
| 3 lines – Tierce | 7 lines – Septet |
| 4 lines – Quatrain | 8 lines - Octave |

## Patterns and Traditions

### Lyric

A lyric is a short poem used to express deep thoughts and emotions about a subject, object, or another person. The content of lyrical poetry is individualized and quite subjective in nature. Formal lyrics include the ballad, the sonnet, and the ode.

#### "Invictus"
Out of the night that covers me,
Black as the pit from pole to pole,
I thank whatever gods may be
For my unconquerable soul.

In the fell clutch of circumstance
I have not winced nor cried aloud.
Under the bludgeonings of chance
My head is bloody, but unbowed.

Beyond this place of wrath and tears
Looms but the Horror of the shade,
And yet the menace of the years
Finds, and shall find me, unafraid.

It matters not how strait the gate,
How charged with punishments the scroll.
I am the master of my fate:
I am the captain of my soul.
                **- William Ernest Henley**

## Ballad

Generally, a ballad is a narrative poem with simple stanzas and a simple rhyme scheme that often contains repetition, dialogue, and a repeated refrain (i.e. a recurrent phrase or series of phrases such as "Quoth the Raven, 'Nevermore'"). Ballads are highly musical poems as many were originally meant to be sung.

The ballad stanza consists of a quatrain with four beats in the first and third lines (iambic tetrameter) and three beats in the second and fourth which also rhyme (iambic trimester). Traditional ballad subjects include murder, love, revenge, shipwrecks, and the supernatural.

from **"The Rime of the Ancient Mariner"**

| | |
|---|---|
| The ice was here, the ice was there, | A |
| The ice was all around : | B |
| It cracked and growled, and roared and howled, | C |
| Like noises in a swound ! | B |

**- Samuel Taylor Coleridge**

## Elegy

An elegy is a formal poem written in lyrical language to commemorate or honor one who has died. "Elegiac" is the adjective describing deep lament for one who is deceased.

from **"Elegy of the Death of John Keats"**

I weep for Adonais - he is dead!
O, weep for Adonais! though our tears
Thaw not the frost which binds so dear a head!
And thou, sad Hour, selected from all years
To mourn our loss, rouse thy obscure compeers,
And teach them thine own sorrow, say: "With me
Died Adonais; till the Future dares
Forget the Past, his fate and fame shall be
An echo and a light unto eternity!"

**- Percy Bysshe Shelly**

## Ode

An ode is a long formal poem written in three parts. The strophe and the antistrophe have a similar rhyme scheme and metrical structure, but they often view the subject of the poem from differing perspectives. The epode has a different scheme and structure and often resolves the issue at hand through synthesis and critical thinking. Odes are often quite meditative in that they deeply analyze an object, person, or idea.

from **"Ode on a Grecian Urn"**

| | |
|---|---|
| Thou still unravished bride of quietness, | A |
| Thou foster child of silence and slow time, | B |
| Sylvan historian, who canst thus express | A |
| A flowery tale more sweetly than our rhyme: | B |
| What leaf-fringed legend haunts about thy shape | C |
| Of deities or mortals, or of both, | D |
| In Tempe or the dales of Arcady? | E |
| What men or gods are these? What maidens loath? | D |
| What mad pursuit ? What struggle to escape? | C |
| What pipes and timbrels ? What wild ecstasy? | E |

- John Keats

## Sonnet

A sonnet is a fourteen-line poem, which is written in iambic pentameter and conforms to a strict formulaic rhyme scheme. Most sonnets contain a rhetorical shift near the end of the poem (usually in the last couplet). There are two main types of sonnets: the Petrarchan (or Italian) and the Shakespearean (or Spenserian):

The **Petrarchan Sonnet** (Italian Sonnet) is adaptable between two basic rhyme schemes: A-B-B-A A-B-B-A C-D-E C-D-E and A-B-B-A A-B-B-A C-D-C D-C-D. The first eight lines of the sonnet are referred to as the "octave" and the last six lines are referred to as the "sestet." The octave exposes a problem, and the sestet solves or analyzes the problem to a greater degree.

### **"The World Is Too Much With Us; Late And Soon"**

| | |
|---|---|
| The world is too much with us; late and soon, | A |
| Getting and spending, we lay waste our powers: | B |
| Little we see in Nature that is ours; | B |
| We have given our hearts away, a sordid boon! | A |
| The Sea that bares her bosom to the moon; | A |
| The winds that will be howling at all hours, | B |
| And are up-gathered now like sleeping flowers; | B |
| For this, for everything, we are out of tune; | A |
| It moves us not.--Great God! I'd rather be | C |
| A Pagan suckled in a creed outworn; | D |
| So might I, standing on this pleasant lea, | C |
| Have glimpses that would make me less forlorn; | D |
| Have sight of Proteus rising from the sea; | C |
| Or hear old Triton blow his wreathed horn. | D |

- William Wordsworth

The **Shakespearean Sonnet** (English Sonnet) is broken into three quatrains and a couplet. A Shakespearian sonnet follows the rhyme scheme of A-B-A-B C-D-C-D E-F-E-F G-G. The couplet often contains a shift where the problem of the poem is resolved in an unexpected way.

### Sonnet 130

| | |
|---|---|
| My mistress' eyes are nothing like the sun; | A |
| Coral is far more red, than her lips red: | B |
| If snow be white, why then her breasts are dun; | A |
| If hairs be wires, black wires grow on her head. | B |
| I have seen roses damasked, red and white, | C |
| But no such roses see I in her cheeks; | D |
| And in some perfumes is there more delight | C |
| Than in the breath that from my mistress reeks. | D |
| I love to hear her speak, yet well I know | E |
| That music hath a far more pleasing sound: | F |
| I grant I never saw a goddess go, | E |
| My mistress, when she walks, treads on the ground: | F |
| And yet by heaven, I think my love as rare, | G |
| As any she belied with false compare. | G |

**- William Shakespeare**

### Questions To Ask
- Has the poet hidden any additional meaning in the particular form she has chosen?
- How does the form of the poem affect its other qualities such as rhythm, tone, etc.?
- What does the form of the poem reveal about the historical setting of the poet's work or the literary period in which it was written?

# Imagery

Imagery is descriptive language that evokes one or more of the five senses (i.e. sight, sound, taste, touch, smell). The goal of literary imagery is to make the reader actually see, feel, taste, touch, or smell the subject or idea at work. Imagery can be produced by using particularly precise, colorful, and active language; by using symbolism; and/or by using figures of speech such as similes, metaphors, and personification.

## Examples

from **"Kubla Khan"**
So twice five miles of fertile ground
With walls and towers were girdled round:
And there were gardens bright with sinuous rills,
Where blossomed many an incense-bearing tree;
And here were forests ancient as the hills,
Enfolding sunny spots of greenery.

**- Samuel Taylor Coleridge**

from **"The Destruction of Sennacherib"**
The Assyrian came down like the wolf on the fold,
And his cohorts were gleaming in purple and gold;
And the sheen of their spears was like stars on the sea,
When the blue wave rolls nightly on deep Galilee.

Like the leaves of the forest when summer is green,
That host with their banners at sunset were seen
Like the leaves of the forest when autumn hath blown,
That host on the morrow lay withered and strown.

**- Lord Byron**

## Questions To Ask

- Is the writing descriptive? Does it contain many sensory details and active verbs, or does it focus more on plot and dialogue?
- Does the reader "see" the story?
- Is the story shown or *told*?
- What senses are brought to life? What images particularly stand out?

# Tone

The general attitude of the author toward the reader or the subject matter of a literary work.

## Tone Vocabulary

| Positive | | | | Neutral | | | Negative | | | | | | |
|---|---|---|---|---|---|---|---|---|---|---|---|---|---|
| **Happy** | **Dignified** | **Sensual** | **Compassionate** | **Honest** | **Funny** | **Ambivalent** | **Sad** | **Indignant** | **Angry** | **Forceful** | **Anxious** | **Aggressive** | **Dark** |
| Airy | Earnest | Desperate | Complimentary | Apologetic | Facetious | Apathetic | Aggrieved | Incredulous | Belligerent | Arrogant | Cautionary | Caustic | Ghoulish |
| Amused | Formal | Hopeful | Concerned | Candid | Farcical | Apprehensive | Depressed | Irrepressible | Bitter | Audacious | Fearful | Critical | Gloomy |
| Animated | Gentle | Intimate | Diplomatic | Confessional | Jovial | Boring | Disheartened | Irreverent | Cold | Callous | Frantic | Disapproving | Grim |
| Bantering | Modest | Passionate | Emotional | Contemplative | Lighthearted | Confused | Distressed | Jaded | Hostile | Condescending | Uneasy | Disdainful | Gothic |
| Carefree | Proud | Reverent | Empathetic | Didactic | Mocking | Cryptic | Disturbed | Malicious | Incensed | Contemptuous | Worried | Disgusted | Sinister |
| Chatty | Restrained | Enthusiastic | | Forthright | Sarcastic | Detached | Emotional | Maniacal | Complaining | Cruel | | Disparaging | |
| Cheerful | Righteous | Loving | | Frank | Satirical | Disbelieving | Funeral | Mean-Spirited | Cynical | Defiant | | Faultfinding | |
| Comic | Tolerant | Obsequious | | Humane | | Evasive | Melancholy | Naïve | | Forceful | | Heartless | |
| Confident | | Sentimental | | Informative | | Impartial | Morose | Patronizing | | Haughty | | Hypercritical | |
| Dreamy | | | | Instructive | | Obtuse | Mournful | Pompous | | Impassioned | | Judgmental | |
| Ecstatic | | | | Introspective | | Skeptical | Pitiful | Provocative | | Imploring | | Outraged | |
| Elated | | | | Matter-of-Fact | | Awestruck | Regretful | Sulking | | Outspoken | | Pessimistic | |
| Euphoric | | | | Nostalgic | | Baffled | Solemn | Affected | | Reproachful | | Resentful | |
| Excited | | | | Objective | | Befuddled | Somber | | | Sarcastic | | Urgent | |
| Exuberant | | | | Philosophical | | Whimsical | Tragic | | | Scornful | | Vindictive | |
| Fanciful | | | | Poetic | | | Ennui | | | Self-righteous | | | |
| Joyous | | | | Doubtful | | | | | | Sharp | | | |
| Playful | | | | Reflective | | | | | | Zealous | | | |
| Witty | | | | Sincere | | | | | | | | | |
| | | | | Thoughtful | | | | | | | | | |

# Symbolism

A symbol is one thing that represents or stands for another. In literature a symbol is generally an object, person, situation, or idea that deepens the meaning of the work by evoking content that is not literally expressed in the work itself.

### Examples
- In Edgar Allan Poe's "The Raven," the raven is thought to be the symbol of a prophet.
- In *The Great Gatsby* the ash in the Valley of Ashes is thought to symbolize both the excrement of the ruling class and the dead dreams of the lower class struggling to survive.
- In *The Adventures of Huckleberry Finn*, Tom Sawyer is said to symbolize society and Romanticism.

### Questions To Ask
- How do the symbols of the piece contribute to its overall meaning? Is there any symbolism present in the names of the characters?
- Are the symbols easy to understand, or are they obscure and opaque?
- Is the piece heavy with symbolism? Why? To what effect?

# Conceit

A conceit is a startling and often unexpected comparison between two wildly dissimilar things. Conceits are often extended metaphors that rely heavily upon imagery and juxtaposition. The"Metaphysical Poets" John Donne, Andrew Marvell, and George Herbert used ingenious conceits to enhance the meaning of their poetry.

### Examples
from **"The Flea"**
Mark but this flea, and mark in this,
How little that which thou deniest me is ;
It suck'd me first, and now sucks thee,
And in this flea our two bloods mingled be.
Thou know'st that this cannot be said
A sin, nor shame, nor loss of maidenhead ;
   Yet this enjoys before it woo,
   And pamper'd swells with one blood made of two ;
   And this, alas ! is more than we would do.
**- John Donne**

from **"A Valediction Forbidding Mourning"**
If they be two, they are two so
As stiff twin compasses are two ;
Thy soul, the fix'd foot, makes no show
To move, but doth, if th' other do. And though it in the centre sit,
Yet, when the other far doth roam,
 It leans, and hearkens after it,
And grows erect, as that comes home.

**- John Donne**

from **"To His Coy Mistress"**
Thy beauty shall no more be found,
Nor, in thy marble vault, shall sound
My echoing song; then worms shall try
That long preserv'd virginity,
And your quaint honour turn to dust,
And into ashes all my lust.

**- Andrew Marvell**

## Questions To Ask
- How does the extended metaphor of the conceit surprise the reader?
- What additional levels of meaning does the conceit provide?
- What part does juxtaposition and/or imagery play in the conceit?
- How does the conceit open new pathways in the mind of the reader?

# Shift

Poets often change their rhetorical stance at some point during their poems. A shift can be essential to the overall meaning of the poem. Sonnets, for example, usually contain a shift somewhere near the last two lines. The sonneteer argues one point for around twelve lines and then suddenly shifts his/her position. Shifts are often preceded by conjunctive phrases such as "and yet," "but then," "however," or "even so."

## Example
In Shakespeare's"Sonnet 73," the shift occurs in the final couplet when the speaker reveals that all of the negative things he has previously said about himself actually make his lover love him more.

## Sonnet 73

That time of year thou mayst in me behold
When yellow leaves, or none, or few, do hang
Upon those boughs which shake against the cold,
Bare ruin'd choirs, where late the sweet birds sang.
In me thou seest the twilight of such day
As after sunset fadeth in the west,
Which by and by black night doth take away,
Death's second self, that seals up all in rest.
In me thou see'st the glowing of such fire
That on the ashes of his youth doth lie,
As the death -bed whereon it must expire
Consumed with that which it was nourish'd by.
   This thou perceivest, which makes thy love more strong,
    To love that well which thou must leave ere long.

**- William Shakespeare**

## Questions To Ask

- At what point in the poem does the shift occur? Why not earlier or later?
- How dramatic is the shift?
- Does the shift negate everything the poet has expressed before, or does it enhance his earlier statements?
- Is the shift subtle or pronounced?
- How does the shift help develop the meaning of the poem?

# Style

Literary style refers to the overall manner or fashion in which an author conveys his or her written message. In the same way that someone's personal style depends upon characteristics such as clothing, stature, movement, speech patterns, attitude, and customs, literary style depends upon characteristics such as diction, syntax, sentences, conventions, tone, and voice"along with every other literary element. Style is more appropriately related to the aesthetics of a piece than to its meaning. Style is often linked historically with the literary period in which the author wrote.

# Meaning

Meaning (i.e. theme or central idea) refers to the core message embedded within a piece of literature. Generally, meaning is a feeling or a philosophical truth that the author hopes to express or better understand. The goal of literary analysis is to extract and explain the meaning of a piece literature. Do this by first breaking the work down into its most effective elements (i.e. imagery, diction, tone, or whatever elements seem to make the most meaning in the piece). Then, explain those elements in detail, with plenty of examples (i.e. supporting details) and commentary (i.e. analysis). Finally, show how those elements fit back together to develop the overall theme or meaning of the piece.

Make sure you answer the "How?" question: How does the work mean what it means? Show how the work means what you say it means by amassing and analyzing a preponderance of evidence for your case.

# Sentences

The type of sentences a piece employs can often have a profound effect on its tone, rhythm, and meaning.

### Simple Sentence
A sentence that contains one independent clause.

### Compound Sentence
A sentence that contains two or more independent clauses joined by a comma and a coordinating conjunction, or by a semicolon.

### Complex Sentence
A sentence that contains one independent clause and one or more dependent clauses (i.e. "subordinate clauses").

### Compound-Complex Sentence
A sentence that contains two or more independent clauses and one or more subordinate clauses.

### Periodic Sentence
A sentence in which the main idea is not understood until the very end of the sentences. A number of dependent clauses and parallel constructions (i.e. parenthetical elements) lead up to the final independent clause or main thought of the sentence.

### Example
> "Whenever I find myself growing grim about the mouth; whenever it is a damp, drizzly November in my soul; whenever I find myself involuntarily pausing before coffin warehouses, and bringing up the rear of every funeral I meet; and especially whenever my hypos get such an upper hand of me, that it requires a strong moral principle to prevent me from deliberately stepping into the street, and methodically knocking people's hats off -- then, I account it high time to get to sea as soon as I can."- Herman Melville - *Moby-Dick*

### Loose Sentence
A sentence in which the main idea can be understood from the very beginning. Usually, the main clause of a loose sentence is followed by an extended list of subordinate clauses.

**Example**

> "I felt an inexpressible relief, a soothing conviction of protection and security, when I knew that there was a stranger in the room, an individual not belonging to Gateshead, and not related to Mrs. Reed."- Charlotte Bronte - *Jane Eyre*

**Questions To Ask**

- Do the sentences contain many subordinate clauses and/or parenthetical elements?
- Do the main clauses usually come at the beginning of the sentences (loose) or at the end of the sentences (periodic)?
- Are there any digressions or interruptions within the sentences?
- Is the word order (syntax) straightforward or unconventionally crafted?
- Are there any unusual techniques, such as stream-of-consciousness, mixing styles and genres, unusual layout on the page, breaking of the rules of grammar and form, or odd or narrative perspectives, etc.?
- Is the writing tight and efficient or elaborate and long-winded?

# Organization

Organization refers to the way a short story, essay, or novel is pieced together. To discuss organization is to discuss the placement and spatial characteristics of the different elements of the work. Some narrative works might be linear in nature (i.e. told from beginning to end). Others may contain flashbacks, flash-forwards, digressions, embedded narratives, and the like. Some rhetorical works may analyze the most important elements of the work first. Others may save the most important arguments for the last portion of the paper.

**Examples**

- Jonathan Safran Foer's *Everything is Illuminated* is told through a series of letters written between a young Ukrainian man and an American Jew, both of whom are engaged in writing their own versions of an adventure they shared while trying to find out the details regarding a lost relative. The actual text of each man's manuscript is included with the letters.
- In "Natural Selection," Charles Darwin uses inductive reasoning to arrive at a general conclusion after the thorough analysis of many specific examples.
- In "Allegory of the Cave" Plato recounts a dialogue between Socrates and Glaucon in which Socrates uses a hypothetical example of cave dwellers identifying shadows on the wall of their cave. Plato uses this allegory to develop an important theme regarding truth, enlightenment, and society's resistance to both.

## Paragraphs

The ordering of paragraphs in a short story or within the chapters of a novel can contribute to an author's style and meaning. The general rule about paragraphs is to devote a new paragraph to each new thought. More numerous paragraphs might indicate more numerous and varying thoughts. In that case, an author's storytelling might be scatterbrained, cursory, or even nebulous, which may be intentional or unintentional.

## Examples

- In Earnest Hemingway's "The Big Two-Hearted River," the narrative unfolds in short, terse paragraphs that accentuate Hemingway's matter-of-fact style and heighten the sense of clarity Nick feels while fishing for trout while immersed in nature.
- *Moby-Dick* contains one chapter titled "The Whiteness of the Whale" in which Herman Melville uses extremely long and complex paragraphs to debunk the traditional notion that whiteness denotes peace, purity, and goodness. The length and complexity of his paragraphs further reinforce the complex, nuanced, and multifaceted idea he is trying to communicate.

## Chapters

If an author employs short and more numerous chapters it might indicate a more expansive novel with varying settings and more intersecting plot lines. Fewer and more pregnant chapters might indicate a more immobile, long-winded piece--one with more well-developed scenes.

## Examples

- *Slaughterhouse-Five* by Kurt Vonnegut is written is short bursts of text that skip wildly throughout the time line of the narrative. Some plot elements are repeated many times. This organizational technique serves to heighten and illustrate a certain view of the universe shared by the Tralfamdorians (an alien race) and perhaps, by the end of the novel, even the reader himself.
- Joseph Conrad's *Heart of Darkness* is told in three parts. Although the work is a novella and quite short in length, each part is extremely long, philosophical, and aesthetically complex.

**Questions To Ask**
- Are the paragraphs very short, or are they enormous blocks of text running across many pages? Are the chapters short or long?
- Do the paragraphs seem to link together logically, or do they shift wildly between loosely connected ideas? How about the chapters? How many chapters/paragraphs are there, and how are they structured? Why is this important?
- What type of reasoning is used, inductive or deductive?

# Delivery

Delivery is the general sense of how a narrative is relayed to the reader. Delivery includes such characteristics as pace, description, and rhythm. To discuss delivery is to discuss the aesthetic qualities of how the story is told or how the rhetorical stance is developed.

**Examples**
- In Charlotte Perkins Gillman's "The Yellow Wallpaper," the narrative unfolds through a series of journal entries. This stream-of-consciousness technique allows Gillman to vary the length of each entry as the narrator slowly looses her grip on reality. By doing this, the reader's anticipation increases as the story's tone slowly becomes more hectic and deranged while the story is progressing toward its climax.
- Mark Twain's *The Adventures of Huckleberry Finn* is delivered through the terse colloquial vernacular of a thirteen-year-old boy. By allowing Huck to tell his own story, Twain is able to use the perspective of an innocent, uneducated child to develop monumentally important themes as Huck slowly unlearns the erroneous lessons with which society has programmed him.
- Martin Luther King Jr. delivers his "Letter from a Birmingham Jail" in the Biblical tradition of Paul who spread the tenets of early Christianity through a series of letters. By using the delivery method of a letter, and one from jail nonetheless, king enhances the power of his rhetoric by targeting his audience specifically and then allowing other readers to eavesdrop on that communication.
- Geoffrey Chaucer's *Canterbury Tales* is a "Frame Story" in which an overall story (an assortment of medieval characters on a pilgrimage to Canterbury Cathedral) is used to set the scene for several shorter stories (the stories of the pilgrims themselves).

**Questions To Ask**
- Is the story told with many "to be" verbs, or is the story shown by allowing details and action to develop what is taking place?
- Does the narrative seem hurried, rushed, or lackadaisical? Or does the author take his or her time recounting even the smallest details of the story?
- Is the writing heavily descriptive, with emphasis on setting and atmosphere, or does it focus on action and plot movement? Does this speed up or slow down the story?
- Does the author use any particular vehicle to deliver the piece (i.e. frame story, letter, etc.)?

# Conventions

Using or not using the proper conventions of grammar can make a bold statement within a text. Many Modernists, for example, turned away from proper conventions in order to convey their feeling that the world is fragmented, disjointed, unorganized, and unruly.

**Examples**
- Cormac McCarthy's *All the Pretty Horses* contains a sentence that is 211 words long and contains fourteen independent clauses, all joined by coordinating conjunctions, but the sentence does not contain a single comma. Also, he spells "blood-red" two different ways in the same sentence. He also spells "don't" two different ways on the same page. One might make the case that by debunking the idea that there is order grammar, McCarthy is reinforcing his theme that there is no order in the universe.
- Earnest Hemingway is famous for writing short, terse, direct sentences in which he uses very few commas. When he does use commas, he uses them according to his own whim rather than standard convention.

**Questions To Ask**
- Does the author use proper grammar, spelling, and punctuation?
- If not, is it a mistake, or does the author intend it as written?
- If mistakes are intentional, why? And, what message do those mistakes send?
- How does intentional grammar misuse develop meaning within the piece?

# Dialogue

Some authors rely heavily on dialogue while others use it only sparingly. The use of dialogue is an important part of a writer's style and can help develop the overall meaning of a piece.

### Examples
- In *Fahrenheit 451* Ray Bradbury develops the main themes of his novel in one lengthy conversation between Montag (the protagonist) and the Beatty (the Captain of the Fire Department).
- In *Heart of Darkness*, Joseph Conrad opens his novella with a long portion of exposition that sets the scene and contains no dialogue. Then, the narrative is taken over by Marlow, another sailor aboard the Nellie who also begins his tale in an expositional manner. Very little dialogue appears until later in Marlow's narrative.

### Questions To Ask
- How often does dialogue, rather than exposition or description, tell the story? Do readers get entire conversations or just fragments?
- Does the conversation use colloquialisms?
- Does one character respond to the questions of another, or does she proceed on to her own thoughts and speech."

# Point of View

Point of view is the perspective from which a work is told. Most basically, there are three different points of view: first person, second person, and third person.

### First Person
In first person point of view the narrator relays the story to the reader as a first-hand account, (i.e. the narrator was a participant or observer in the story and is now relaying what he/she actually saw, heard, or felt). In first person point of view, personal pronouns are used (e.g. I, me, we, us, etc.).

In fiction prose, first person is often thought to be the most powerful way to tell a story. It provides closeness between the action and the narrator and the narrator can directly relay the thoughts and feelings he or she had at the time of the action. Therefore, readers are truly inspired when Huck Finn finally proclaims, "All right then, I'll go to hell." He says this in his own voice rather that having that message relayed through a detached and impartial narrator.

For non-fiction essays, first person is generally to be avoided. First person often makes rhetoric seem colloquial and biased. Rhetorical compositions should read like textbooks (i.e. written from an impartial third-person observer).

## Second Person

In second person point of view, the narrator or writer addresses the reader as "you." Second person is generally to be avoided altogether. A composition that relies heavily on second person ends up sounding preachy and offensive.

## Third Person

In third person point of view, a detached narrator tells the story in an objective manner. No first-person or second-person pronouns are used (i.e. I, me, we, you, us, etc.). Third person point of view generally comes in three varieties:

### Omniscient

An omniscient narrator tells a story with complete and unrestricted knowledge. An omniscient narrator knows the internal thoughts and feelings of every character involved in the narrative. This type of narrator can move freely between different geographic locations (i.e. divulge simultaneous events that are happening at multiple locations which are separated by vast distances). Omniscient narrators can also move freely in time, relaying past, present, and future events.

### Limited

Third person limited point of view occurs when a narrator filters her story through the perspective of only one character. The narrator can still convey that character's internal thoughts and feelings, but all other characters must be developed through the viewpoint of the central character.

### Objective

In third person objective point of view, a narrator has the freedom to move in space and time, but he can only relay action and dialogue, forgoing the ability to delve into characters' thoughts and feelings. Third person objective point of view is much like the perspective of most films where a camera records the action and dialogue of the story, but there is no intruding narrative voice and no editorializing," just the facts.

**Questions To Ask**
- How does the author's choice of point of view affect the style of the piece?
- How does the author's choice of point of view affect the meaning of the piece?
- Does the point of view shift?
- Are there multiple points of view? If so, what effect does this have on the piece?

# Characterization

Generally, characterization refers to the different ways an author can choose to describe and develop the characters in her work. There are two primary methods of characterization:

### Direct
The narrator comments directly on the attributes of the character (e.g. "He was a funny guy").

### Indirect
The narrator shows the attributes of the character by placing him or her in situations by which the reader can judge what kind of person he is (e.g. "Jason wiggled his ears, and his classmates broke into laughter").

Discuss characters and characterization by analyzing such attributes as physical appearance, personality, background/personal history, motivation, relationships, internal conflicts, etc. Also, is the character static (i.e. she remains the same throughout the work) or dynamic (i.e. he changes throughout the course of the narrative).

### Types of Characters
- **Antagonist:** The character in the work who brings about the conflict. The antagonist is generally the"bad guy."
- **Confidante:** A character who is usually used as a device to indirectly develop the protagonist. A confidante is the recipient of privileged information from the main character.
- **Dynamic Character:** A character who undergoes a change over the course of the narrative. The conflict and plot of the story affects a dynamic character and elicits a change within him.
- **Flat character:** A stereotypical, stock, or cardboard character. A flat character is usually one-dimensional, static, and shallow (although often

well-defined).

- **Foil:** A character whose attributes contrast with those of the protagonist, thereby serving to heighten or accentuate the characteristics of the protagonist.
- **Narrator:** The actual person who is telling the story can also be a character within the story itself. This is often the case in first-person narratives.
- **Protagonist**: The main character of the narrative. The protagonist is generally the central character of the work and the character who is primarily involved in the main conflict of the story.
- **Round Character:** A character who is complex, nuanced, and multifaceted. Round characters stand in contrast to flat characters in that they are not stereotypical and often surprise readers with unexpected behavior and values.
- **Static Character:** A character who does not change throughout the course of the narrative. A static character is the same at the end of the work as he was at the beginning.
- **Archetype:** A prototype character that is instantly and universally understood by all readers. Consider the following archetypes: the sage, the mentor, the hero, the devil (or personification of evil like Darth Vader), the trickster, the mother, the temptress, the friend, etc.
- **Sympathetic Character:** A character with whom readers can identify. Sympathetic characters are usually well liked by readers, even though sympathetic characters can sometimes be evil.
- **Unsympathetic Character:** A character with whom readers cannot identify. Unsympathetic characters are often villains whose values run contrary to social norms and who almost always have nefarious intentions.

## Questions To Ask
- What is a particular character's motivation?
- With what is a particular character struggling, internally or externally?
- Does a particular character surprise readers? Or is she dull and uninspiring?
- How do most readers feel about a particular character? Positive or negative?
- Which character is most affected by the main conflict of the narrative?
- How does the author choose to reveal the attributes of her characters?
- How do the actions and motivations of the characters develop the meaning of the piece?

# Setting

The setting of a narrative is the physical and temporal backdrop in which the story takes place. Setting involves not only geography and time but also characteristics such as political climate, social mores, weather, proximity to historical events, occupation of the characters, etc. Authors often use the setting of a work to create, heighten, or further illustrate the main conflict of the story.

### Questions To Ask
- Is the setting an integral part of the narrative or simply the scenery?
- Is the story timeless or does it depend on a temporal setting?
- Does the setting constitute a pathetic fallacy (i.e. does the setting reveal the internal emotions of one or more of its characters?

# Conflict

The conflict of a story is the main clash, argument, disagreement, discord, or problem faced by the protagonist. There are several types of conflicts:

- **Internal conflict or person-against-self:** The protagonist struggles with opposing forces, emotions, beliefs, and/or values with himself.
- **Interpersonal conflict or person-against-person:** The protagonist struggles against another person or entity.
- **Person-against-society:** The protagonist struggles against the values, mores, and/or condition of the society in which she lives.
- **Person-against-nature:** The protagonist struggles against the elements of nature or natural forces beyond human control.
- **Person-against-fate:** The protagonist struggles against a condition prescribed by fate (e.g. a disability, an accident, a death, etc.).

### Questions To Ask
- Is there only one conflict, or are there several conflicts that are deeply intertwined and synthesize themselves into an even larger, more complex problem?
- How does the resolution (or irresolution) of the conflict help develop the overall meaning of the work? What effect does the conflict have on the characters in the story?
- Does an internal conflict cause the protagonist to change in some fundamental way?

# Details

As overlooked of an element as it may seem, an author's choice of detail is an essential part of storytelling. Close reading is all about attention to detail. Often small, subtle details can determine the overall meaning of a work. When responding to prose, scrutinize every sentence and every word of a piece to find out what might be hidden in plain sight.

### Questions To Ask
- Does anything seem strange or out of place? Is there anything extra?
- Are there long-winded descriptions? If so, why spend so much energy on that one thing?

# Anecdotes

An anecdote is a short story told within the broader context of a rhetorical piece. Anecdotes can be very effective rhetorical devices as they often draw readers in and provide excellent emotional (pathetic) appeals.

### Examples
- A mother might tell the tragic story of her son being killed by a drunk driver before she launches into her logical and ethical reasons why a new law should be enacted.
- A woman might relay the gruesome story of her own botched liposuction surgery in a letter to the state Medical Board demanding additional licensing requirements for doctors who perform the procedure.

### Questions to Ask
- Is the anecdote shown with sensory details, or is it told with flat ambiguous language?
- Is the anecdote relevant to the overall rhetorical aim of the paper?
- Does the anecdote overpower the entire paper, or is it just the right length to do the trick?
- Does the anecdote ring true, or does the reader get the sense that it is made up?
- What overall effect does the anecdote have on the meaning of the piece?

# Ethos, Logos, Pathos

Ethos, Logos, and Pathos (ethics, logic, and emotion) are the three principle appeals used in most persuasive, argumentative, and rhetorical pieces.

**Ethos -** An appeal to ethics. Also, ethos is sometimes attributed to the fact that an authority in a given field has a greater ability to persuade on topics concerning her own expertise.

### Examples
- Nine out of ten dentists agree . . .
- It is morally wrong to allow others to starve while we have so much.

**Logos -** An appeal to logic. Logical appeals rely upon rationality for their effectiveness.

### Examples
- "If all your friends jumped off of a bridge, would you?"
- "Because there is a creation, there must be a creator"- Deist axiom

**Pathos -** An appeal to emotion. The goal of an emotional appeal is to tug on reader's heartstrings.

### Examples
- For just ten cents a day . . .
- An anecdotal war story told from the perspective of a child.

### Questions To Ask
- Does the author mix appeals? Which appeal is most effective?
- Does the intended audience match the author's choice of appeal?
- Are the appeals well executed or poorly developed?

# Irony

In a general sense, irony is a contradiction between what is expected and what actually occurs, or it is a contradiction between what is said and what is actually meant. There are three basic types of irony: verbal, situational, and dramatic.

**Verbal Irony** - When an author or speaker says exactly the opposite of what he/she means.

## Examples
- "I can think of no one objection that will probably be raised against this proposal . . ."
- Jonathan Swift - "A Modest Proposal" (On the proposition of selling impoverished Irish infants to English Lords who would consume them as a delicacy.)
- Oh, it didn't surprise me in the least to hear this, and at the same time to be told that Fresleven was the gentlest, quietest creature that ever walked on two legs. No doubt he was; but he had been a couple of years already out there engaged in the noble cause, you know, and he probably felt the need at last of asserting his self respect in some way." - Joseph Conrad - *Heart of Darkness*

**Situational Irony** - When the reality of a situation differs or seems opposite from what is expected.

## Examples
- "But Tom Sawyer he hunted me up and said he was going to start a band of robbers, and I might join if I would go back to the widow and be respectable." - Mark Twain - *The Adventures of Huckleberry Finn*
- "In the shallows, face downward, lay the oiler. His forehead touched sand that was periodically, between each wave, clear of the sea."- Stephen Crane -"The Open Boat" (The oiler, "Billie," is the most noble and hard -working character in the story. He is the only casualty.)
- "You? Impossible! A mason ?" "A mason," I replied.
  "A sign," he said.
  "It is this," I answered, producing a trowel from beneath the folds of my roquelaire." Edgar Allan Poe "The Cask of Amontillado"

**Dramatic Irony -** When the reader or audience knows more about the situation than the actual characters in the work.

### Examples
- In Charlotte Perkins Gillman's "The Yellow Wallpaper" the reader knows that the narrator is mad and delusional before she knows it herself.
- At the end of William Shakespeare's Romeo and Juliet, the audience knows that Juliet has taken a sleeping potion and is not really dead. Romeo, unfortunately, does not know this vital information.

## Assonance

The repetition of vowel sounds.

### Examples
- "In Xanadu did Kubla Khan" - Samuel Taylor Coleridge (The a and u sounds repeat.)
- Hear the mellow wedding bells - Golden bells!
- What a world of happiness their harmony foretells! Through the balmy air of night
- How they ring out their delight! - From the molten - golden notes, And all in tune,
- What a liquid ditty floats
- To the turtle - dove that listens, while she gloats
- On the moon!
- Edgar Allan Poe "The Bells" (The o sound repeats.)
- And so, all the night-tide, I lie down by the side / Of my darling, my darling, my life and my bride. - Edgar Allan Poe "Annabel Lee" (The i sound repeats.)

## Personification

When humanlike qualities are given to objects or animals.

### Examples
- "As if this earth in fast thick pants were breathing," - Samuel Taylor Coleridge "Kubla Khan"
- "Smile O voluptuous cool-breath'd earth! . . . Smile, for your lover comes." - Walt Whitman "Leaves of Grass"
- "There was never a sound beside the wood but one, / And that was my long scythe whispering to the ground." - Robert Frost "Mowing"

**Anthropomorphism -** A type of personification that occurs when animals or non-human objects come alive as if they were human and become characters in a literary work.

**Examples**
- Consider the animals who come to life and rule the farm in George Orwell's *Animal Farm.*
- Consider the White Rabbit and the Cheshire Cat in Lewis Carroll's *Alice in Wonderland.*

# Alliteration

Repetition of consonant sounds.

**Examples**
- "It was while gliding through these latter waters that one serene and moonlight night, when all the waves rolled by like scrolls of silver; and, by their soft, suffusing seethings, made what seemed a silvery silence, not a solitude: on such a silent night a silvery jet was seen far in advance of the white bubbles at the bow." - Herman Melville - *Moby-Dick*
- "The summer soldier and the sunshine patriot will, in this crisis, shrink from the service of their country; but he that stands by it now, deserves the love and thanks of man and woman." - Thomas Paine
- "If God should only withdraw his hand from the flood-gate, it would immediately fly open, and the fiery floods of the fierceness and wrath of God, would rush forth with inconceivable fury, and would come upon you with omnipotent power." - Jonathan Edwards - "Sinners in the Hands of an Angry God"

# Repetition

Reusing the same words or phrases for rhythmic or rhetorical effect.

**Examples**
- "We must fight! I repeat it, sir, we must fight!" - Patrick Henry - "Speech to the Virginia Convention"
- "If I am going to be drowned--if I am going to be drowned--if I am going to be drowned, why, in the name of the seven mad gods who rule the sea, was I allowed to come thus far and contemplate sand and trees?" Stephen Crane "The Open Boat" (The whole sentence is also repeated throughout the story.)

# Paradox

When two contradictory items exist simultaneously.

### Examples
- "I adore simple Pleasures," said Lord Henry."They are the last refuge of the complex."- Oscar Wilde - *The Picture of Dorian Gray*
- "Conscience and cowardice are really the same things, Basil. Conscience is the trade-name of the firm." - Oscar Wilde - *The Picture of Dorian Gray*
- "Cowards die many times before their deaths."- William Shakespeare

# Hyperbole

Exaggeration to an extreme degree.

### Examples
- "Always! That is a dreadful word. . . . Women are so fond of using it. They spoil every romance by trying to make it last forever. . . . The only difference between a caprice and a life-long passion is that the caprice lasts a little longer."- Oscar Wilde - *The Picture of Dorian Gray*
- "Trade and commerce, if they were not made of India rubber, would never manage to bounce over obstacles which legislators are continually putting in their way; and, if one were to judge these men wholly by the effects of their actions, and not partly by their intentions, they would deserve to be classed and punished with those mischievous persons who put obstructions on the railroads."- Henry David Thoreau - "Resistance to Civil Government"
- "The question before the House is one of awful moment to this country. For my own part, I consider it as nothing less than a question of freedom or slavery;"- Patrick Henry - "Speech to the Virginia Convention"

# Rhetorical Question

A question that is asked with the purpose of making the reader think, thus persuading him/her toward the author's cause.

### Examples
- "Don't you know the devilry of lingering starvation, its exasperating torment, its black thoughts, its somber and brooding ferocity?"- Joseph

Conrad - *Heart of Darkness*
- "Did he who made the lamb make thee?"- William Blake - "The Tyger"
- "Why should they begin digging their graves as soon as they are born ?"- Henry David Thoreau - *Walden*

# Parallelism

Using like grammatical structure, diction, and phrasing to correlate clauses and phrases, both within and among sentences and paragraphs.

## Examples
- "To strive, to seek, to find, and not to yield." - Alfred, Lord Tennyson - "Ulysses"
- "One morning, in cool blood, I slipped a noose about its neck and hung it to the limb of a tree; - hung it with the tears streaming from my eyes, and with the bitterest remorse at my heart; - hung it because I knew that it had loved me," - Edgar Allan Poe - "The Black Cat"
- "We have petitioned; we have remonstrated; we have supplicated; we have prostrated ourselves before the throne,"- Patrick Henry - "Speech to the Virginia Convention"
- "The drover watching his drove sings out to them that would stray,
  The pedler sweats with his pack on his back, (the purchaser higgling about the odd cent;)
  The bride unrumples her white dress, the minute -hand of the clock moves slowly,
  The opium-eater reclines with rigid head and just-open'd lips," - Walt Whitman - "Song of Myself"

# Metaphor

Comparing two things without using the words "like" or "as."

## Examples
- "Yet all experience is an arch wherethrough / Gleams the untraveled world whose margin fades / Forever and forever when I move." - Alfred, Lord Tennyson - "Ulysses"
- "Gather ye rosebuds while ye may, Old time is still a-flying; / And this same flower that smiles today, tomorrow will be dying."- Robert Herrick - "To the Virgins, to Make Much of Time."
- "All visible objects, man, are but pasteboard masks." - Herman Melville - *Moby-Dick*

- "Standing on the bare ground - my head bathed by the blithe air, and uplifted into infinite space,"all mean egoism vanishes. I become a transparent eyeball. I am nothing. I see all. The currents of the Universal Being circulate through me; I am a part or particle of God." - Ralph Waldo Emerson - "Nature"
- "A foolish consistency is the hobgoblin of little minds, adored by little statesmen and philosophers and divines."- Ralph Waldo Emerson - "Self-Reliance"

# Allusion

A reference to something outside of the text to produce rhetorical or stylistic effect. For maximum effect, allusions should refer to items that are a part of the collective consciousness, such as the Bible, Shakespeare, or mythology.

## Examples
- "Suffer not yourselves to be betrayed with a kiss."- Patrick Henry - "Speech to the Virginia Convention"
- "The Burial of the Dead" - Title of T.S. Eliot's first section of "The Waste Land" (Allusion to The Book of Common Prayer of the Anglican Church of England)

# Simile

Comparing two things using "like" or "as."

## Examples
- "And whilst our souls negotiate there, / We like sepulchral statues lay;"- John Donne - "The Ecstasy"
- "The wrath of God is like great waters that are dammed for the present; they increase more and more, and rise higher and higher, till an outlet is given; and the longer the stream is stopped, the more rapid and mighty is its course, when once it is let loose."- Jonathan Edwards -"Sinners in the Hands of an Angry God"
- "Our two souls therefore, which are one, Though I must go, endure not yet A breach, but an expansion, Like gold to airy thinness beat." - John Donne - "A Valediction: Forbidding Mourning"

# Style

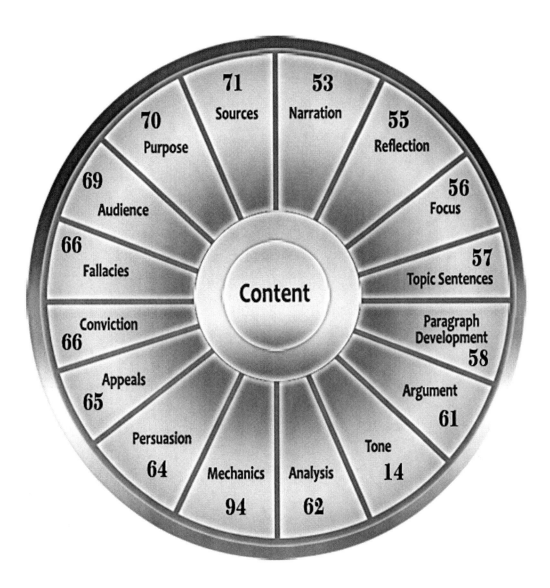

# Content

# Organization

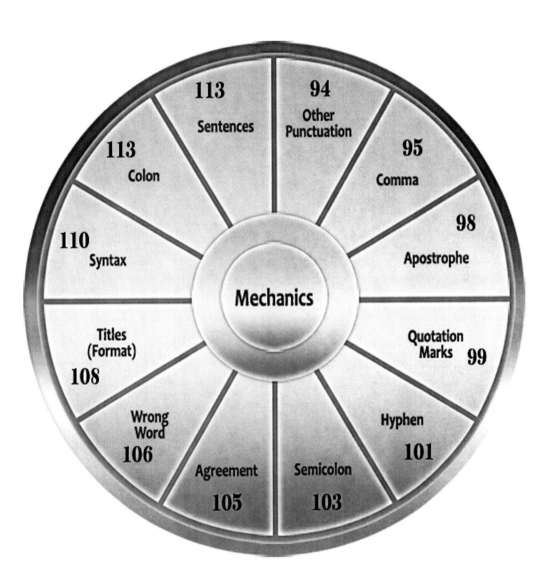

# Mechanics

# Readability

Work on the fluency and flow of your writing. Great ideas can often be lost in a paper with mechanical errors, awkward syntax, poor organization, and difficult phrasing.

## Factors To Consider

1. Carefully edit and proofread your paper.
2. If English is not your first language, pay special attention to verb forms and verb tenses. For a paper that flows and reads well, it is very important to use verbs correctly.
3. Ask a friend to read your paper and circle any awkward portions that do not seem to flow. Use transitions to indicate shifts and connections between ideas.
4. Vary your sentence types for a more fluid style. Do not rely too heavily on one type of sentence. Mix it up with a variety of simple, complex, compound, and compound-complex sentences.
5. Vary your sentence beginnings in order to prevent a sense of choppy repetition. To bring variety to your sentence beginnings, use the words and phrases below to begin introductory clauses (with a comma afterward):
    - after,although
    - in as much as, as if, as though, because
    - before
    - even if, even though, if
    - in order that, providing that, provided that, now that, once
    - seeing as how, seeing that, since
    - so, so that, though, unless, until
    - when, whereas, wherever
    - no matter where, when, why, etc., whenever
    - however, whichever, whoever, whosoever, whatever
6. Read your paper aloud after every revision to make sure it flows and that you have actually written what you intended to write.
7. Work on developing a unique and well-defined voice. Delete all cliches and colloquialisms from your writing.
8. Do not write your essay the same way you speak. Academic essays should be written in formal scholarly language.
9. Write in the tense and point of view that is appropriate for the assignment.
10. Usually, academic essays should be written in third person (i.e. do not use I, me, we, us, etc.). When writing about literature, use the literary present tense.

# Diction

Diction refers to the type of words a writer chooses (i.e. vocabulary). Sometimes, diction can be characterized as high, middle, or low, depending on the degree of sophistication and formality of the words used. Mark Twain is famous for saying, "The difference between the right word and the almost right word is the difference between lightning and a lightning bug." Diction has a profound effect on the quality, style, and meaning of an essay.

Employ effective diction by first deciding what type or types of words will be of most benefit to the development of your rhetorical purpose. Then decide how those types of words can help to develop tone, emotion, and meaning.

## Examples

- *Moby-Dick* contains a chapter titled "The Try-Works" in which Herman Melville uses words like "fierce," "Tartarean," "pagan," "pronged poles," "hissing," "scalding," "snaky flames," "boiling," "scorched," "tawny," "begrimed," "barbaric," "fire," "red hell," and "emblazonings" to evoke feelings and images of hell, evil, horror, and torment.
- In "After great pain, a formal feeling comes," Emily Dickinson uses words like "Tombs," "stiff," "mechanical," "Wooden," "Quarts," "stone," and "lead" in order to convey a feeling like the heavy, unnatural, and gradual hardening sensation one feels after a great heartbreak.

# Sentences

The type of sentences a writer employs can often have a profound effect on the tone, rhythm, flow, readability, and meaning of his or her essay. Vary the length and type of sentences you use in order to enhance the fluency and flow of your writing and enhance the overall rhetorical effectiveness of your essay.

**Simple Sentence -** A sentence that contains only one independent clause (IC).

## Examples

- I hit the ball.
- The problem is trust and honesty.
- I hit the ball and ran the bases.
- My car skidded out of control.

**Compound Sentence -** A sentence that contains two or more independent clauses joined by a comma and a coordinating conjunction (or by a semicolon).

## Examples
- I hit the ball, and I ran the bases.
- My car skidded out of control, and we hit the guardrail.
- My car skidded out of control, and we hit the guardrail, but that is what saved our lives.

**Complex Sentence -** A sentence that contains one independent clause and one or more dependent clauses (i.e. DC or "subordinate clause").

## Examples
- Because it was the last game of the season, I hit the ball.
- Because it was the last game of the season, I hit the ball as hard as I could.
- Although we still don't know why, my car skidded out of control.
- If you love fishing so much, you should buy a boat.
- I bought my boat because I love fishing so much.

**Compound-Complex Sentence -** A sentence that contains two or more independent clauses and at least one dependent clause.

## Examples
- Because it was the last game of the season, I hit the ball, and I ran the bases.
- Because it was the last game of the season, I hit the ball as hard as I could, but it was a foul.
- Although we still don't know why, my car skidded out of control, and we hit the guardrail.
- Although we still don't know why, my car skidded out of control, and we hit the guardrail, but that is what saved our lives.
- If you love fishing so much, you should buy a boat, but you shouldn't buy anything you can't afford.
- I bought my boat because I love fishing so much, and that was the best decision I ever made.

**Periodic Sentence -** A sentence in which the main idea is not understood until the very end of the sentence. A number of dependent clauses and parallel constructions (i.e. parenthetical elements) lead up to the final independent clause or main thought of the sentence.

**Example**

"Whenever I find myself growing grim about the mouth; whenever it is a damp, drizzly November in my soul; whenever I find myself involuntarily pausing before coffin warehouses, and bringing up the rear of every funeral I meet; and especially whenever my hypos get such an upper hand of me, that it requires a strong moral principle to prevent me from deliberately stepping into the street, and methodically knocking people's hats off -- then, I account it high time to get to sea as soon as I can." - Herman Melville - *Moby-Dick*

**Loose Sentence -** A sentence in which the main idea can be understood from the very beginning. Usually, the main clause of a loose sentence is followed by an extended list of dependent clauses.

**Example**

"I felt an inexpressible relief, a soothing conviction of protection and security, when I knew that there was a stranger in the room, an individual not belonging to Gateshead, and not related to Mrs. Reed." Charlotte Bronte - Jane Eyre

# Works Cited

A "Works Cited" page is a list of sources that were actually used within an essay. A "Bibliography" page is a list of sources that might possibly be used in an essay.

1. Organize your Works Cited page alphabetically by author or by the first word of the citation if there is no author.
2. Retain the same font, margins, and line spacing as used in the body of the essay.
3. Indent the second and subsequent lines of each citation.

Below is a list of the most common types of MLA citations. Consult the MLA Handbook for additional models and more detailed information.

### Book with One Author

Shanafelt, Colin. *What Gods Would Be Theirs?*. Austin: Gatsby's Light
    Publications, 2011. Print.

### Book with Multiple Authors

Smith, Paula, and Jim Latamer. *How To Live a Good Life.* London: Saxon Press,

2000. Print.

Samson, Joe, et al. *The Art of Conversation.* New York: Vintage, 1917. Print.

*Use "et al." for three or more authors. Et al. is the Latin abbreviation for and others.*

### Work from an Anthology

Pinker, Steven. "Thinking Machines." *A World of Ideas: Essential Readings for College Writers.* Ed. Lee A. Jacobus. Boston: Bedford/St. Martin's, 2010. 528-49. Print.

Atwood, Margaret. "Rape Fantasies." *Fiction 100: An Anthology of Short Stories.* 13th ed. Ed. James H. Pickering. Boston: Pearson, 2012. 31-37. Print.

### Journal Article (Print)

Cardeiro, Jose. "The Singularity Is Nigh." *Engineering and Technology* 5.1 (2010): 27-29. Print.

### Journal Article (Web Database)

Aguero, Martin, et al. "Artificial Intelligence for Software Quality Improvement." *The World Academy of Science: Engineering and Technology* 63.1 (2010): 234-39. *Academic Search Complete.* Web. 30 Sept. 2010.

### Web Article

Kharif, Olga. "Artificial Intelligence Goes Mobile." *SFGate.com.* San Francisco Chronicle, 27 Sept. 2010. Web. 30 Sept. 2010.

# Voice

The term voice refers to the unique sound and feel of your prose. A writer's voice is created by his style--the way he uses almost every element of literature (i.e. tone, sentences, diction, figures of speech, mechanics, etc.). Developing a unique, well-defined, and effective voice is a goal that many writers struggle to achieve for their entire lives. After reading your essay, the reader should feel like she knows you, she should understand the nuances of your tone and personality, and she might even be able to close her eyes and envision you as an authentic flesh-and-blood person rather than a dry emotionless scribe.

**Factors To Consider**

- Be authentic. Readers can easily detect "faking it" or apathy toward a topic.
- Have conviction. Never use constructions like "I feel," "some believe," "I believe," or "in my opinion." These phrases make it seem as if you are walking on eggshells and trying not to offend anyone (or be wrong).
- Read your work aloud. Many times writers get so bogged down in the composition of an essay that, after the paper is complete, it has ceased to sound like anything they would ever write.
- Work on your readability, fluency, and flow. These attributes will often help develop a more effective voice.

# Point of View

Point of view is the perspective from which an essay is told. Most basically, there are three different points of view: first person, second person, and third person. Academic essays are often required to be written in third person (i.e. without the use of personal pronouns such as I and me).

**First Person -** In first person point of view, the writer relays the essay to the reader as a first-hand account, (i.e. the writer was a participant or observer in the action and is recounting what she actually saw, heard, and felt). In first person point of view, personal pronouns are used (e.g. I, me, we, us, etc.). For non-fiction essays, first person is generally to be avoided. First person often makes a writer's rhetoric seem colloquial and biased. Most academic essays should read like textbooks (i.e. written from an impartial third-person observer).

**Examples**
- "Where I Lived and What I Lived For" by Henry David Thoreau
- "Shooting an Elephant" by George Orwell

**Second person -** In second person point of view, the narrator or writer addresses the reader as "you." Second person is generally to be avoided. A composition that relies heavily on second person ends up sounding preachy and offensive.

**Third Person -** In third person point of view, a detached writer relays information in an objective manner. No first-person or second-person pronouns are used (i.e. I, me, we, you, us, etc.). Most serious academic essays are written in third person point of view. Interjecting your own thoughts and feelings into an academic essay should be generally avoided. When an academic essay is written in first person, the essay quickly becomes more about the writer rather than the actual topic of the essay. Narrative third person point of view comes in three general varieties: omniscient, limited, and objective.

### Omniscient

An omniscient narrator tells a story with complete and unrestricted knowledge. An omniscient narrator knows the internal thoughts and feelings of every character involved in the narrative. This type of narrator can move freely between different geographic locations (i.e. divulge simultaneous events that are happening at multiple locations separated by vast distances). Omniscient narrators can also move freely in time, relaying past, present, and future events at will.

### Limited

Third person limited point of view occurs when a detached narrator filters her story through the perspective of only one character. The narrator can still convey that character's internal thoughts and feelings, but all other characters must be developed through the viewpoint of the central character.

### Objective

In third person objective point of view, a narrator has the freedom to move in space and time, but he can only relay action and dialogue, forgoing the ability to delve into characters' thoughts and feelings. Third person objective point of view is much like the perspective of most films where a camera records the action and dialogue of the story, but there is no intruding narrative voice and no editorializing, just the facts.

### Examples
- "The Mystery of Dark Matter" by Michio Kaku
- "Of the Natural Progress of Opulence" by Adam Smith

# Tense

Be very careful to use the proper tense for the proper purpose, and take care not to erroneously mix tenses.

**Simple Present -** The action is happening now.
- She sings.

**Present Perfect -** Although the action started in the past, that action continues into the present and/or future. Present perfect tense is created with a past participle and a present perfect verb.
- She has sung.

**Simple Past -** The action happened in the past and has now concluded.
- She sang.

**Past Perfect -** The action began in the past and continued for an extended period but has now ceased. Past perfect tense is created with a past tense helping verb and a present perfect verb.
- She had sang.

**Future -** The action will happen in the future.
- She will sing.

**Future Perfect -** The action will begin in the future and will last for an extended period of time but will eventually cease.
- She will have sung.

### Literary Present

When writing about literature, write in present tense, unless the action you are writing about happened before the narrative begins. The idea here is that from now until the end of time anyone who picks up a specific work will read the exact same story. Therefore, the action is always happening in the present.

### Examples
- Jim and Huckleberry Finn float down the river.
- Most people believed that Huck's father had been dead for a long time.

### Universal Laws

Write all universal laws in the present tense.

### Examples
- Gravity works very well.
- Shakespeare is the greatest writer of all time.
- I think, therefore I am.

### Tense Errors

Be careful to avoid errors in tense.

### Examples (Errors)
- Bill lost his wallet. He said he leaves it in a cab.
- The students realized that their homework was due in two weeks.
- All humans were created equal. (Universal Truth - "are")
- Fortunato was walled up in the catacombs by Montressor. (Use literary present.)

# Format

Format your essay as per the instructions given to you by your teacher or professor. If no guidelines were given, always default to the standard MLA paper format below:

- **Margins -** 1 inch on top, bottom, and sides
- **Font -** Times New Roman 12 pt. throughout (no exceptions)
- **Spacing -** double space your entire paper
- **Heading -** name, professor's name, assignment name, and date in upper left corner (double spaced)
- **Title -** an original title (not the title of the assignment) centered on the first page on the first line below heading, no bolding, no italics, no font change
- **Page numbers -** your last name and the page number in the header, right justified (not on first page)
- **Justification -** left, not full or right (no blocked text)
- **Binding -** Staple your pages together.
- **Cover Page -** Do not use a cover page.
- **Paragraph Spacing -** Do not skip extra lines between paragraphs. Double-space the entire paper. Paragraph indentations - 1/2 inch.
- **Sentence Spacing -** Space only once between sentences.
- **Point of View -** Unless specifically authorized, do not use the first or second person point of view (I, you, we, us).

# Delivery

Delivery is the general sense of how the information in an essay is relayed to the reader. Delivery includes such characteristics as style, organization, pace, description, rhythm, and methods of development. Deliver your essay by whatever means is most appropriate to your audience and rhetorical purpose.

### Examples
- Jonathan Swift's "A Modest Proposal" is delivered as a satire.
- Mark Twain's "Two Views of the River" is delivered as a first-person narrative contrasting what the Mississippi river meant to him at two different times in his life.
- Molly Ivins's "Get a Knife, Get a Dog, but Get Rid of Guns" is delivered as a humorous op-ed piece.
- Michael Levin's "The Case for Torture" uses a hyperbolic hypothetical situation as the premise for its overall rhetorical assertion.

# Figures of Speech

A figure of speech is any language that is used in a non-literal way or for rhetorical effect.

1. **Irony** - In a general sense, irony is a contradiction between what is expected and what actually occurs, or it is a contradiction between what is said and what is actually meant. There are three basic types of irony - verbal, situational, and dramatic.
   - **Verbal Irony** - When an author or speaker says exactly the opposite of what he/she means.
   - **Situational Irony** -When the reality of a situation differs or seems opposite from what is expected.
   - **Dramatic Irony** - When the reader or audience knows more about the situation than the actual characters in the work.
2. **Personification** - Giving humanlike qualities to objects or animals.
3. **Alliteration** - The repetition of consonant sounds.
4. **Repetition** - Reusing the same words or phrases for rhythmic or rhetorical effect.
5. **Paradox** - When two contradictory items exist simultaneously.
6. **Hyperbole** - Exaggeration to an extreme degree.
7. **Rhetorical Question** - A question that is asked with the purpose of making the reader think, thus persuading him/her toward the author's cause.
8. **Parallelism** - Using like grammatical structure, diction, and phrasing to correlate clauses and phrases, both within and among sentences and paragraphs.
9. **Metaphor** - Comparing two things without using the words "like" or "as."
10. **Allusion** - A reference to something outside of the text in order to produce rhetorical or stylistic effect. For maximum effect, allusions should refer to items that are a part of the collective consciousness, such as the Bible, Shakespeare, or mythology.
11. **Simile** - Comparing two things using "like" or "as."

# Narration

Tell your story in the best, most suspenseful way possible. Lure the reader into your narrative with a hook--an exciting, imaginative introduction to seize your reader's attention. Then, SHOW the story through specific sensory and action details. Do not just tell the reader what happened; make the reader a witness to the action. Use specific sensory details (sight, sound, taste, touch, and smell) along with powerful nouns and active verbs to bring your narrative alive.

SHOW. Don't tell.

Be specific, definite, and concrete. Never speak in general or ambiguous terms. The woman is not "pretty." The word pretty is a general term that can be interpreted in many ways. Thus, pretty means nothing. Pretty does not describe a single attribute about the woman, nor does it excite any of the five senses. When writing, always remember to use imagery to draw your reader into the narrative. Telling a story in ambiguous terms makes your reader lose interest (the kiss of death).

Take extreme care to develop your ideas fully. To mention an idea only briefly is to rob it (and your essay) of its vitality and nuance.

Finally, narrow your topic down to something that you can fully develop in an essay of the required length. Essays that are too broad end up reading more like lists rather than stories.

## Do
- Provide a catchy hook at the beginning of your narrative in order to seize the reader's attention. Be specific versus general.
- Use imagery and sensory details.
- Spend more energy describing action than setting.
- Narrow the scope of your essay in order to fully develop the narrative. Start in the middle of the story rather than at the beginning.
- Show the reader what your characters are like through action.

## Do Not
- Do not include details that do not enhance the story or your message.
- Do not start the narrative too early in the sequence of events. Start with the main action. Do not spend too much energy describing setting.
- Do not tell your story; SHOW it! Do not speak in general terms.

**Examples**

The hatch, removed from the top of the works, now afforded a wide hearth in front of them. Standing on this were the Tartarean shapes of the pagan harpooners, always the whale-ship's stokers. With huge pronged poles they pitched hissing masses of blubber into the scalding pots, or stirred up the fires beneath, till the snaky flames darted, curling, out of the doors to catch them by the feet. The smoke rolled away in sullen heaps. To every pitch of the ship there was a pitch of the boiling oil, which seemed all eagerness to leap into their faces. Opposite the mouth of the works, on the further side of the wide wooden hearth, was the windlass. This served for a sea-sofa. Here lounged the watch, when not otherwise employed, looking into the red heat of the fire, till their eyes felt scorched in their heads. Their tawny features, now all begrimed with smoke and sweat, their matted beards, and the contrasting barbaric brilliancy of their teeth, all these were strangely revealed in the capricious emblazonings of the works. As they narrated to each other their unholy adventures, their tales of terror told in words of mirth; as their uncivilized laughter forked upwards out of them, like the flames from the furnace; as to and fro, in their front, the harpooners wildly gesticulated with their huge pronged forks and dippers; as the wind howled on, and the sea leaped, and the ship groaned and dived, and yet steadfastly shot her red hell further and further into the blackness of the sea and the night, and scornfully champed the white bone in her mouth, and viciously spat round her on all sides; then the rushing Pequod, freighted with savages, and laden with fire, and burning a corpse, and plunging into that blackness of darkness, seemed the material counterpart of her monomaniac commander's soul. **- Herman Melville - Moby-Dick**


This second night we run between seven and eight hours, with a current that was making over four mile an hour. We catched fish and talked, and we took a swim now and then to keep off sleepiness. It was kind of solemn, drifting down the big, still river, laying on our backs looking up at the stars, and we didn't ever feel like talking loud, and it warn't often that we laughed -- only a little kind of a low chuckle. We had mighty good weather as a general thing, and nothing ever happened to us at all -- that night, nor the next, nor the next.

Every night we passed towns, some of them away up on black hillsides, nothing but just a shiny bed of lights; not a house could you see. The fifth night we passed St. Louis, and it was like the whole world lit up. In St. Petersburg they used to say there was twenty or thirty thousand people in St. Louis, but I never believed it till I see that wonderful spread of lights at two o'clock that still night. There warn't a sound there; everybody was asleep.
**- Mark Twain - *The Adventures of Huckleberry Finn***

# Reflection

Many instructors prefer essays that connect the primary topic of the essay to history, life, or the world today. To reflect upon a topic is to learn something from it, to grow, to synthesize, to take something away. A good general reflection moves a topic from abstract ideas to a concrete lesson. To reflect upon a topic is to answer the "So what?" question. You may have explained every detail of a topic, but "So what?" What does it all mean? What is the life lesson that you and your readers can take away from it?

## Factors To Consider

- An effective reflection is generally positioned at the very end of a paper.
- A reflection is a type of conclusion or result; make sure your reflection actually follows from the content and arguments of your essay.
- To avoid losing credibility, take care that your reflection is not a non sequitur or overly dramatic.

## Example

In *All the Pretty Horses*, Cormac McCarthy rejects the grand narrative that there is order in the universe. He regards humanity's greatest fallacy to be our common belief that the universe is organized, meaningful, and under intelligent control. *All the Pretty Horses* is his manifesto against this fallacy and other high ideals of its kind. For McCarthy the universe is absurd. It does not make sense. It is not under any type of intelligent control. Thus, there is only a short distance between McCarthy's limited proposition and the argument's ultimate conclusion: When we perceive life and the universe to make sense, we make our decisions based upon false assumptions. When we see the universe as a place of clearly defined good and evil--a black and white universe--the result is violence, war, chaos, and unrest. One man's orderly universe is another man's fairy tale. Therefore, under the perception of an orderly, controlled universe, all sides see themselves as right. Perceptions diverge, tempers flare, and wars begin. Therefore, the idea of universal order and divine justice is not only an illusion, as McCarthy warns, but it is the very thing that resigns our world to the pangs of hate and tribal war.

# Focus

Beware of off-topic / off-thesis writing. Every word in your paper should directly relate to the overall topic of your essay as identified in the thesis statement. Likewise, every word in each of your paragraphs should directly relate to that paragraph's topic sentence.

## Scope

- Reduce the scope of your essay in order fully develop your ideas and stay on-topic. Do not try to do too much. When a topic is too broad, an essay often ends up looking more like a laundry list of vague details and broad generalities than an in-depth critical analysis.
- Narrow down your topic by subdividing it into as many parts as you can. Is one of those parts a more appropriate topic for the length of the essay you are assigned? If so, consider modifying your topic.
- Another way to reduce your scope is to limit your audience and rhetorical purpose. If you are writing for a well-educated audience, there may be less need to define terms and include background details.
- Instead of explaining an entire concept and persuading your readers to act, you might consider writing only a referential essay in which you explain the concept in an unbiased way.
- For narrative essays, reduce your scope and develop important ideas more fully. Start in the middle of the action. If your essay is about a ski trip, there is no need to begin your story at the airport. Rather, begin on the slopes where the main action of the story commences.

## Outlining

- Writing a detailed and comprehensive outline is one of the most important and effective things you can do to remain focused within an essay (and to enhance the quality of just about every other aspect of your essay).
- Write your outline before you begin writing your essay.
- Write and edit your thesis statement first. List your full thesis in your outline.
- Write and edit your topic sentences in your outline. List your full topic sentences.
- Gather the evidence you will use in each paragraph. Briefly catalog each piece of evidence in your outline and note where to find it.
- Spend up to 1/3 of your writing time on perfecting your outline. Having a great outline makes writing an essay much less difficult.

**Factors To Consider**
- Delete any information, analysis, evidence, or argumentation that does not directly relate to and support the assertion you make in your thesis statement.
- Carefully read your topic sentence. Does everything in that paragraph directly support the point you make in your topic sentence?
- If your paragraph is actually about something else, then modify your topic sentence.
- If your paragraph contains ideas that are not expressed within or signaled by its topic sentence, then delete those portions from your essay or analyze them in paragraphs of their own.

# Topic Sentences

The first sentence of every paragraph is its topic sentence. A topic sentence is an explicit controlling statement that explains exactly what the entire paragraph will be about.

**Factors To Consider**
- Every topic sentence must directly relate to the essay's thesis statement by proving or developing one aspect of the assertion or point made within that thesis.
- All content within a paragraph should directly support the point or assertion made in the topic sentence. Any writing that does not directly support a paragraph's topic sentence should be deleted or examined in a paragraph of its own.
- Topic sentences should be exceptionally clear, direct, and well written.
- A reader should be able to understand an essay's general topic, argument, and meaning after reading only its thesis and the first sentence of every paragraph (topic sentences).
- Think of topic sentences as the main points of your argument. For example, if your thesis asserts that the death penalty is unconstitutional, your topic sentences will state the several reasons why.

**Do**
- Use topic sentences to support your thesis. Topic sentences should explain or develop one aspect of the idea you asserted in your thesis statement.
- Place your topic sentence at the beginning of every paragraph, the first sentence.
- Use your topic sentence to directly state what that paragraph will cover.

**Do Not**

- Do not begin a paragraph with a question or a quotation.
- Do not bury your topic sentence in the middle of a paragraph.
- Do not lead up to your topic sentence at the end of a paragraph.
- Do not write topic sentences that fail to directly support your essay's thesis statement.

**Examples**

- Congress is now considering tough new internet privacy laws in order to protect consumers who want to feel safe about using their computers at home to conduct business and shop online.
- With the goal of offering fifth generation (5G) services before 2013, wireless companies are currently scrambling to develop new technologies for mobile devices and the wireless web.
- In order to increase profits and help curb the rising cost of medical insurance in the United States, private companies are now collecting and archiving the personal medical information of American citizens without those patients' knowledge or consent.
- Attention Deficit/Hyperactivity Disorder (ADD) is the most common childhood psychiatric condition in the Unites States today.

# Paragraph Development

An effective paragraph should be developed with a clear argument, ample evidence, and plenty of scholarly analysis. Each paragraph should illustrate or prove only one idea. Writing a paragraph is like proving a case in court. The topic sentence is like the overall plea (Not Guilty); the evidence is like the objective, unquestionable data collected from an original source (DNA, fingerprints, alibi, etc.); and the scholarly analysis is like the lawyer's explanation of why a certain piece of evidence proves the that defendant is not guilty.

1. **Topic Sentence (TS) -** a clear, direct, and comprehensive statement explaining what the paragraph will be about; makes an assertion that the paragraph will prove
2. **Evidence (EV) -** a direct quotation, fact, statistic, example, case study, experiment, expert opinion, anecdote, etc.
3. **Analysis (AN) -** commentary, argument, and explanation as to why a piece of evidence proves the assertion made in the topic sentence

*\*\*In order to write a fully developed paragraph, some writers find it helpful to adhere to the following pattern - TS - EV - AN - EV - AN.\*\**

A developed paragraph might contain two pieces of evidence, each accompanied by strong, convincing analysis. But a ***well-developed*** paragraph might contain three or more pieces of evidence along with plenty of highly convincing analysis. A poorly developed paragraph can suffer from a lack of evidence, a lack of analysis, or both.

## Poorly Developed

In "Sonnet 129" William Shakespeare explains the dangers of human desire. Throughout the sonnet, Shakespeare's language seems rushed. This makes readers feel a sense of urgency, a feeling much like the desire or lust he is warning against. Next, the poet explains that extreme desire makes a person "mad" (Shakespeare 8). And because of that madness, even when a person gets what he wants, he cannot enjoy it. He has become like an animal--unable to reason. So instead of enjoying his conquest, he merely finds something else to pursue.

## Well Developed

In "Sonnet 129" William Shakespeare uses forced meter, evocative diction, and the fading distinction between humanity and beasts to illustrate the idea that humans go mad in the pursuit of--and eventually in the possession of--the objects they desire. Shakespeare's sonnet charges into motion with forced meter in its first line: "Th' expense of spirit in a waste of shame" (Shakespeare 1). The syllables "th'" and "ex" rush together forming a line of iambic pentameter out of what would otherwise be eleven syllables of thought. Thus, from the poem's very inception, the reader feels a sense of eagerness and begins to anticipate the sonnet's larger theme of barbaric lust and desire. Next, the poet goes on to explain that until one achieves the object of his lust, he is "murderous," "bloody," "full of blame," "rude," "cruel," and "savage" (3-4). These highly suggestive words evoke images of Machiavellian-style brutality and reinforce the idea that when one covets, he becomes uncivilized and feral. He is willing to do anything--even beyond the boundaries of his own ethics--to attain the object of his affection. But Shakespeare takes his argument to its ultimate conclusion by explaining that even after an enchanted object has been attained, it is not "bliss" that follows but "woe" (11). Once conquered, that man, woman, material object, or entity which was once so desperately pursued becomes despised and hated. There is much truth to the old axiom that "People always want what they cannot have." This is why the things in our actual possession rarely provide any lasting sense of happiness or relief. Finally, the objects for which we lust, Shakespeare explains, are "Past reason" (6); they exist in an absurd realm of foolishness and insanity. Therefore, lust brings one to madness and thereby destroys the chief distinction between humanity and animals: reason. The ability to reason is vital to the human condition--part of that same human "spirit" Shakespeare venerates in his very first line. So, to desire and covet is to murder one's own vitality, one's own spirit, and one's own humanity. When we lust, we become like animals--beasts who cannot enjoy our conquests, even in victory. We have lost all reason and perspective, and we merely set our sights on a new object of desire and continue our mad, never-ending pursuit for happiness.

## Illustrated Example

- Topic Sentence (TS) - **Bold Underlined**
- Evidence (EV) - Underlined
- Analysis (AN) - ***Bold Italics***

<u>**In "Sonnet 129" William Shakespeare uses forced meter, evocative diction, and the fading distinction between humanity and beasts to illustrate the idea that humans go mad in the pursuit of--and eventually in the possession of--the objects they desire.**</u> <u>Shakespeare's sonnet charges into motion with forced meter in its first line : "Th' expense of spirit in a waste of shame" (Shakespeare 1).</u> ***The syllables "th'" and "ex" rush together forming a line of iambic pentameter out of what would otherwise be eleven syllables of thought. Thus, from the poem's very inception, the reader feels a sense of eagerness and begins to anticipate the sonnet's larger theme of barbaric lust and desire.*** <u>Next, the poet goes on to explain that until one achieves the object of his lust, he is "murderous," "bloody," "full of blame," "rude," "cruel," and "savage" (3-4).</u> ***These highly suggestive words evoke images of Machiavellian-style brutality and reinforce the idea that when one covets, he becomes uncivilized and feral. He is willing to do anything--even beyond the boundaries of his own ethics--to attain the object of his affection.*** <u>But Shakespeare takes his argument to its ultimate conclusion by explaining that even after an enchanted object has been attained, it is not "bliss" that follows but "woe" (11).</u> ***Once conquered, that man, woman, material object, or entity which was once so desperately pursued becomes despised and hated. There is much truth to the old axiom that "People always what they cannot have." This is why the things in our actual possession rarely provide any lasting sense of happiness or relief.*** <u>Finally, the objects for which we lust, Shakespeare explains, are "Past reason" (6);</u> ***they exist in an absurd realm of foolishness and insanity. Therefore, lust brings one to madness***

*and thereby destroys the chief distinction between humanity and animals: reason. The ability to reason is vital to the human condition--part of* that same human "spirit" Shakespeare venerates in his very first line. *So, to desire and covet is to murder one's own vitality, one's own spirit, and one's own humanity. When we lust, we become like animals--beasts who cannot enjoy our conquests, even in victory. We have lost all reason and perspective, and we merely set our sights on a new object of desire and continue our mad, never-ending pursuit for happiness.*

# Argument

The overall effectiveness of an essay often hinges upon the rhetorical strength of its arguments. With that in mind, follow the guidelines below to construct strong, clear, convincing, and well-developed arguments.

1. Use a robust thesis statement to explicitly state the position you will argue and the several articles of proof you will use to back it up.
2. Write a strong topic sentence at the beginning of every paragraph that clearly states the argument that paragraph will make in support of the thesis statement.
3. Supply ample evidence to support your claims. Evidence can come in many forms, but some of the most common types of evidence include the following:
    - **Facts**
    - **Statistics**
    - **Examples**
    - **Case Studies**
    - **Experiments**
    - **Expert Opinions**
    - **Anecdotes**
4. Develop each paragraph / argument with at least two pieces of evidence.
5. Fully analyze and explain why each piece of evidence supports, illustrates, or proves the assertion made in the topic sentence (which in turn supports the assertion made in the thesis statement).
6. Use the most effective appeals for the intended audience of your essay (i.e. ethos, logos, pathos).
7. Accommodate the views, tastes, and needs of your audience.
8. For maximum persuasive impact, consider employing one or more of the following techniques within your argument:
    - **Value Judgments**

- A Call To Action
- Comparisons and Contrasts
- Definitions and Illustrations

9. Clarify your argument by establishing a logical chain of reasoning.
10. Deal with opposing viewpoints by anticipating, addressing, and refuting your opponent's objections. Then, show those arguments to be invalid, flawed, weak, false, biased, or unfair.
11. Make appropriate use of inductive and deductive reasoning.

## Deductive Reasoning

Moves from a general premise to a specific conclusion:

**Syllogism** - a major premise, a minor premise, and a conclusion
- Major Premise - The U.S. Constitution grants citizens the right to own firearms. (A=B)
- Minor Premise - A pistol is a firearm. (B=C)
- Conclusion - U.S. citizens have the right to own pistols. (A=C)

## Inductive Reasoning

Moves from a specific case to a general rule:

**Question/Hypothesis**

Why does the earth's average temperature continue to rise?

**Evidence**

1. Earth's increase in temperature has drastically accelerated in the last one hundred years.
2. Humanity has produced energy by burning fossil fuels mostly within the last one hundred years.
3. The burning of fossil fuels produces gasses that trigger the greenhouse effect.
4. The greenhouse effect causes the earth's average temperature to rise.

**Conclusion**

Earth's increase in temperature is caused by burning fossil fuels.

# Analysis

Analysis makes up the core of your overall argument. It is largely upon the strength or weakness of your analysis that your rhetorical goal will succeed or fail. Generally, analysis is used to illustrate why a piece of evidence proves, supports, or develops the assertion made in a topic sentence (which in turn supports the assertion made in the thesis statement).

**Factors To Consider**
- Use high-level scholarly logic in the analysis portions of your paper.
- After every piece of evidence you cite, provide ample scholarly analysis to prove why that evidence proves the point you are making.
- Use analysis to clarify nuances and complicated ideas.
- Lengthen and clarify the analytical portions of your paper in order to make your paper longer and more effective.

**Illustrated Example** - (Analysis in ***Bold Italics***)

- Topic Sentence (TS) - **Bold Underlined**
- Evidence (EV) - Underlined
- Analysis (AN) - ***Bold Italics***

**In "Sonnet 129" William Shakespeare uses forced meter, evocative diction, and the fading distinction between humanity and beasts to illustrate the idea that humans go mad in the pursuit of--and eventually in the possession of--the objects they desire.** Shakespeare's sonnet charges into motion with forced meter in its first line - "Th' expense of spirit in a waste of shame" (Shakespeare 1). ***The syllables "th'" and "ex" rush together forming a line of iambic pentameter out of what would otherwise be eleven syllables of thought. Thus, from the poem's very inception, the reader feels a sense of eagerness and begins to anticipate the sonnet's larger theme of barbaric lust and desire.*** Next, the poet goes on to explain that until one achieves the object of his lust, he is "murderous," "bloody," "full of blame," "rude," "cruel," and "savage" (3-4). ***These highly suggestive words evoke images of Machiavellian-style brutality and reinforce the idea that when one covets, he becomes uncivilized and feral. He is willing to do anything--even beyond the boundaries of his own ethics--to attain the object of his affection.*** But Shakespeare takes his argument to its ultimate conclusion by explaining that even after an enchanted object has been attained, it is not "bliss" that follows but "woe" (11). ***Once conquered, that man, woman, material object, or entity which was once so desperately pursued becomes despised and hated. There is much truth to the old axiom that "People always what they cannot have." This is why the things in our actual possession rarely provide any lasting sense of happiness or relief.*** Finally, the objects for which we lust, Shakespeare explains, are "Past reason" (6); ***they exist in an absurd realm of foolishness and insanity. Therefore, lust brings one to madness and thereby destroys the***

*chief distinction between humanity and animals: reason. The ability to reason is vital to the human condition--part of* <u>that same human "spirit" Shakespeare venerates in his very first line.</u> *So, to desire and covet is to murder one's own vitality, one's own spirit, and one's own humanity. When we lust, we become like animals--beasts who cannot enjoy our conquests, even in victory. We have lost all reason and perspective, and we merely set our sights on a new object of desire and continue our mad, never-ending pursuit for happiness.*

# Persuasion

Persuasion is an argument that calls readers to action. When we persuade our parents, family, or friends, we are always trying to get them to do or believe something. The same is true of persuasion within an essay.

## The Rhetorical Triangle

Persuasion (rhetoric) can be represented as a triangle with author, audience, and purpose at its three points.

**Author** - As the writer of the essay, you may need to develop some credibility with your audience.
- What are your qualifications to write the essay?
- Do you have any special knowledge, experience, or education that lends credibility to you as the author of this essay?
- Have you previously conducted research on this topic?
- Have you written or published any prior works on this subject?

**Audience** - In order to effectively persuade your readers, you need to understand exactly who they are. Once you have identified and analyzed your intended audience, you must specifically tailor your arguments, persuasive appeals, style, format, and tone for maximum effectiveness with that group of individuals. Identify and analyze your audience based on the following questions:

- Who will read my paper?
- Who am I trying to call to action with this essay? What is my relationship with them?
- What is their level of knowledge and interest in this subject? What are their preconceived notions about the subject?
- How will they respond to my arguments?

**Purpose -** Writing and essay without first explicitly identifying your purpose is like driving away in a car with no destination in mind. If you do not know where you are going, you will never get there. Answer these questions:

- Do you wish to share your emotions about a topic? (**Express**)
- Do you wish to convey specific information? (**Inform**)
- Do you wish to convince your reader of something? (**Argue**)
- Do you wish to call your readers to action? (**Persuade**)
- Do you wish to tell a story? (**Narrate**)
- Do you wish to examine, study, or investigate something? (**Analyze**)

# Persuasive Appeals

Ethos, Logos, and Pathos (i.e. ethics, logic, and emotion) are the three principle appeals used in most persuasive, argumentative, and rhetorical pieces.

**Ethos -** An appeal to ethics. Also, ethos is sometimes attributed to the fact that an authority in a given field has a greater ability to persuade on topics concerning her own expertise.

### Examples
- Nine out of ten dentists agree . . .
- It is morally wrong to allow others to starve while we have so much.

**Logos -** An appeal to logic. Logical appeals rely upon rationality for their effectiveness.

### Examples
- "If all your friends jumped off of a bridge, would you?"
- "Because there is a creation, there must be a creator"- Deist axiom

**Pathos -** An appeal to emotion. The goal of an emotional appeal is to tug on reader's heartstrings.

### Examples
- For just ten cents a day . . .
- An anecdotal war story told from the perspective of a child.

### Questions To Ask
- Does the author mix appeals? Which appeal is most effective?
- Does the intended audience match the author's choice of appeal?
- Are the appeals well executed or poorly developed?

# Conviction

Have some conviction for your side of the argument. Make a stand. Be firm. Convince your reader that you actually know and agree with your own stance.

Phrases like "I believe," "some people think," and "in my opinion," together with words like "may" and "seem" show a lack of confidence and conviction. You are the one writing the essay; now is your time to tell the reader how it is. Plant a flag in the ground and take a definitive stance.

### Examples
- "In my opinion, global warming is a man-made phenomenon." (Lack of Conviction)
- "Global warming is a real, scientifically proven, man-made phenomenon that is currently affecting our world in many horrendous ways."

# Logical Fallacies

A fallacy is an argument that contains misleading, erroneous, or contradicting logic. Logical fallacies are usually the result of false assumptions and misconceptions.

**Ad Hominem -** Attacking the person rather than the argument itself.

### Examples
- You may say that tax cuts simulate the economy, but you are just following a fad. (ad hominem abusive)
- Your position on abortion is wrong because you are a man and can't

possibly understand. (ad hominem circumstantial)
- I might pay more attention to your argument if you weren't such a blonde. (ad hominem abusive)

**Bandwagon -** Using the number of people who support a position as proof of its validity.

### Examples
- Over 75% of the people in this country believe in ghosts, so you should too.
- Almost everybody believes Americans should be able to carry concealed firearms. How could they all be wrong?
- All my friends smoke pot, so it can't be that bad.

**Begging the Question -** Using the premise of an argument as its proof.

### Examples
- The Bible is the word of God because it says so in "Leviticus."
- I'm telling the truth. That's how you know I'm not lying.
- The reason he is a glutton is because he eats too much.

**False Analogy -** Assuming that because two things are alike in one way they must be alike in others.

### Examples
- These two cars are about the same size and color, so they should both be pretty reliable.
- George W. Bush and Rick Perry are both born-again Christians. Therefore, their leadership styles will be about the same.

**False Authority -** Assuming that an expert in one field is equally reputable in another.

### Examples
- Jeffery Williams, Harvard Professor of Molecular Biology, supports the proposed ban on same-sex marriage.
- Sally has a PhD in English, and she believes the U.S. should invest heavily in renewable energy.

**False Cause -** Assuming that because one event followed another the first event caused the second.

### Examples
- Mayor Williams took office, and our city's economy plunged into recession.
- Since Congress passed the concealed carry law, shootings have tripled.

**False Dilemma** - Presenting a complex argument as having only two possible solutions (either / or fallacy).

### Examples
- If we do not fight the British, we will all be slaves.
- We have to either outlaw same-sex marriage or allow people to marry their dogs and cats.

**Hasty Generalization -** Making a grand, sweeping conclusion based on too little evidence.

### Examples
- Elderly people are really bad drivers.
- All feminists hate men.

**Non Sequitur -** Making a conclusion that does not follow from the premise of the argument.

### Examples
- Wealthy Americans are getting richer and richer; therefore, tax cuts must stimulate the economy.
- The Catholic Church is the richest private organization on the planet, so God must exist.

**Red Herring -** Drawing attention away from the substance of an argument to focus on something unrelated.

### Examples
- Why worry about the applicant's criminal record when we know that he attends church every Sunday.
- I know I wrecked the car, but if you had taught me how to drive correctly this wouldn't have happened.

**Slippery Slope** - Assuming that if one thing is allowed then a catastrophic collapse will follow.

### Examples
- Once the government has the power to censor one type of art, it won't be long before the government is censoring all human communication.
- If gays and lesbians are allowed to marry, the next thing you know people will be marrying their toasters.

# Audience

Think very carefully about your intended audience. For maximum literary and rhetorical effectiveness, vary your style, tone, form, and methods of development for your essay's intended audience. Just as we would not speak to our parents and professors in the same manner as we would speak to our peers, as an essay writer, you must know and understand the specific person or group of people who will read your essay. Analyze your audience, and address your intended readers in the most effective way possible.

### Factors To Consider
- Values
- World view
- Age
- Background
- Education level
- Geographic region
- Ethnicity
- Needs and interests

### Questions To Ask
- What is your relationship with them?
- Are they sympathetic or hostile to your views?
- What is their level of knowledge regarding the subject
- Which persuasive appeals will they find most convincing (i.e. ethos, logos, pathos)?
- Which types of evidence will they find most convincing (i.e. facts, quotations, statistics, studies, expert testimony, etc.)?

# Purpose

Write your essay with a specific rhetorical purpose in mind. Great essays focus on achieving a particular goal and never stray from that commitment.

## Expressive

The purpose of an expressive essay is to communicate your thoughts, feelings, ideas, or point of view. Expressive essays are most often developed with narration, description, and evaluation. Expressive essays are considered less scholarly because they are often subjective in nature, they are rarely documented with highly credible sources, and they are frequently written in first person point of view.

## Examples
- "Where I Lived and What I Lived For" by Henry David Thoreau
- "Beauty: When the Other Dancer Is the Self" by Alice Walker
- "Shooting an Elephant" by George Orwell

## Referential

The purpose of a referential essay is to explain, analyze, or inform the reader about a specific topic. Referential essays can be developed in may ways including cause and effect, comparison and contrast, classification, description, definition, exemplification, and process analysis. Referential essays are objective in nature. They focus on the topic at hand and do not contain opinions, editorial content, persuasion, or personal expressions. Referential essays are quite scholarly. They often read like textbooks and are often supported with highly credible source material, such as peer- reviewed journal articles.

## Examples
- "Politics and the English Language" by George Orwell
- "The Climate Emergency" by Al Gore
- "The Qualities of the Prince" by Niccolo Machiavelli

## Interpretive

The purpose of an interpretive essay is to translate the characteristics and meaning of a subject into new and perhaps clearer terms. Interpretive essays can be developed by a variety of means including cause and effect, comparison and contrast, classification, description, definition, exemplification, and process analysis. Interpretive essays are best employed when a writer seeks to bring further clarity to a complex subject.

**Examples**
- "The Mystery of Zen" by Gilbert Highet
- "On Being a Cripple" by Nancy Mairs

**Persuasive**
The purpose of a persuasive essay is twofold: 1. To convince readers that one side of a particular argument is more true, correct, moral, or sensible than the other (i.e. argumentation) 2. To call readers to action in favor of that chosen side. Persuasive essays can employ all patterns of development.

**Examples**
- "Self-Reliance" by Ralph Waldo Emerson
- "Letters from a Birmingham Jail" by Dr. Martin Luther King Jr.

# Sources

Most effective academic essays are developed with evidence from highly credible sources. However, a simple Google search might return millions of potential sources for your essay topic. Therefore, it is crucial to evaluate the relevance and credibility of your sources.

## Types of Sources

**Primary** - These are the original materials that relate to your essay topic. They have not been edited, evaluated, changed, or tampered with. For example, if you are writing about the U.S. Constitution, the U.S. Constitution itself will be your primary source. Primary sources provide the best kind of evidence. Some types of primary sources are as follows:
- Diaries / Journals
- Original Letters and E-mails
- Interviews
- Photographs
- Speeches
- Artifacts
- Birth Certificates
- Court Transcripts
- Works of Art

**Secondary** - These are accounts, interpretations, criticism, and evaluations written or produced after the primary sources. Secondary sources have filtered, evaluated, and changed the original topic. Therefore, secondary sources are discussions, commentaries, and analyses of evidence rather than evidence itself. Some types of secondary sources are as follows:

- Encyclopedias
- Wikipedia
- Magazine, Newspaper, and Journal Articles
- Website Pages and Articles
- Textbooks
- Biographies
- Histories

## Evaluating Sources

### Source Requirements

1. **Relevant** - Sources should be recent or up-to-date and should support the assertion made in your thesis statement.
2. **Representative** - Sources should include all aspects, sides, facts, and points of view regarding your specific topic.
3. **Credible** - Sources should be free from bias, conflicts of interest, demagoguery, poor source material, and weak arguments. Credible sources are written by respected authors, published by respected organizations, and they often contain valid research and evidence from highly credible sources

### Checking for Bias

- Does the author treat opposing views fairly?
- Is the argument hyperbolic or one-sided?
- Does the source's author or publisher endorse a special interest group?
- Does the author use political or religiously biased speech?
- Does the author or publisher have a conflict of interest (i.e. do they stand to gain anything from the outcome of the debate)?
- Is ideologically charged rhetoric apparent?

### Assessing the Argument

- Is the author's argument well developed and supported with highly credible sources?
- Does the author's argument hinge upon any logical fallacies?
- Does the author base her conclusions on a questionable premise?
- Is the evidence relevant, representative, sufficient, and used fairly?

## Source Credibility Ranking

1. Primary Sources
2. Peer-Reviewed Journal Articles
3. Studies and Research Findings (from major organizations and universities)
4. Books (with credible authorship and sponsorship)
5. Articles and Reports (from major media organizations)
6. Web pages (from major media organizations)

***Never cite Wikipedia, Sparknotes, Cliff's Notes, personal web pages, blogs, Facebook, etc.***

# Arrangement

The arrangement of an essay refers to its overall organizational structure. An essay's arrangement is often determined by its rhetorical purpose (i.e. referential, narrative, persuasive, etc.). There are many ways to arrange an essay, but some of the more common methods are as follows:

1. **Description** - Examines the specific details of a subject in order to fully depict and explain it.
2. **Illustration** - Uses one or more specific examples to prove a point.
3. **Cause and Effect** - Evaluates the causal relationships at play within a given subject.
4. **Comparison and Contrast** - Analyzes the similarities and differences of two or more topics.
5. **Classification and Division** - Breaks a subject down into its elemental parts and examines the nature of those parts.
6. **Problem and Solution** - Scrutinizes a given issue and proposes a resolution.
7. **Analogy** - Compares a given subject to another unrelated and more widely known subject.
8. **Definition** - Extends the definition of a term in order to fully explain an idea or concept.
9. **Narration** - Tells a story in order to develop an overall main idea.

## Do

- Choose the appropriate arrangement for the appropriate task.
- Organize your essay for maximum rhetorical effectiveness with the specific arrangement you have chosen.

## Do Not

- Do not force your essay into an arrangement that is inappropriate for its topic.
- Do not signal that you will write in one arrangement and then stray away from that format.

## Questions To Ask

- Is your essay organized according to the conventions of the format you have chosen?
- Does your arrangement strengthen your rhetorical effectiveness?
- Have you stayed true to the arrangement you have chose for the entirety of the paper?

# Introduction

An essay's introductory paragraph should seize the reader's attention and spark interest in the topic to be discussed. A good introduction is crucial, for it is upon the merit of this paragraph that readers will first judge the overall quality of the essay. An essay's introduction provides its first impression. A negative first impression can be very hard to overcome.

In general, the introductory paragraph should provide a hook (see "Hook" within this guide); any background information necessary to understand the topic; a clearly stated explanation of the main problem, scenario, text, topic, or subject the essay will cover; the various sub-categories, classes, or aspects of the topic to be covered; and a strong thesis (controlling statement) that governs the entire essay by explicitly stating what the paper will cover, discuss, or prove. The thesis statement should be the last sentence in the introductory paragraph and should be able to stand alone as a coherent thought without the aid of any other information in the introductory paragraph (see "Thesis" within this guide).

## Do

- Provide a catchy hook at the beginning of your introduction in order to seize the reader's attention. Provide any background information and/or explanatory comments needed to set up the topic.
- Explain the problem or topic to be covered and identify any sides, sub-structures, or organizing elements that may be pertinent to it.
- Clearly express what the paper will discuss, cover, or prove. Although, try not to steal your own thunder by being too explicit; try to dangle the topic before your reader, withholding your main points until later in order to encourage your reader to continue.
- Include an exceptionally well-written thesis as the last sentence of the introductory paragraph.
- Establish the tone of the essay. The particular tone you convey in your essay should be pronounced and perhaps even exaggerated in your introduction. The tone of the introduction should be sustained throughout the entire essay.
- Literary Analysis Essays - List the author's full name and the title of the work to be analyzed. Clearly state the work's central idea (i.e. theme or meaning) and perhaps a few brief comments about how that theme connects to our world today.

**Do Not**

- Do not begin your essay with a quotation. The first character of your essay should not be a quotation mark. All quotations must be introduced and explained.
- Do not begin your essay with a question. This is a technique used in lower-level essays in order to spark creativity in the writer. But on more advanced levels, opening with a question seems a bit corny or patronizing. Do not make important arguments in your introduction. Save important content for dedicated paragraphs or more appropriate places within the body of your essay.
- Do not use too many concrete details (i.e. quotations, paraphrases, examples, details, etc.) in your introduction. Save your primary evidence for later paragraphs.
- Do not be long-winded in your introduction. This paragraph should be interesting, fluent, confident, and comprehensive enough to prepare your reader to understand the paper's topic, but it should not be long and tedious. Your introduction should be powerful but brief. The introductory paragraph should be around 200 to 250 words in length.

## Examples

The drudgery of every human intellectual enterprise from the first thinker to the scholars of our day has been assumed in order to untangle the very same enigma. Every artist, scholar, scientist, and theologian, each in his own way, hopes to illuminate something transcendent, beautiful, and true. The Irish poet William Butler Yeats was no exception. The world stretched out before him as a world not of plain objects to be known in and of themselves, but as a world of mystical subjects--symbols that carry the transcendence and truth which so many great thinkers have sought. He saw symbolism as the greatest conductor of human emotion, and hidden within that emotion, "that modulation of mystic energy," he saw universal truth (Yeats 234). Poetry, and the symbolism within it, was to Yeats as the laboratory is to the chemist, as the pulpit is to the priest, or as the search engine is to the scholar, for he believed that only through literary symbolism can we evoke universal truth and come to know the "god it calls before us" (Yeats 247)

Walter Van Tilburg Clark's "The Portable Phonograph" illustrates the fragility of human culture and warns of how easily we may lose that culture due to our own destructive tendencies. Culture is what separates mankind from animals. It is the collected intellectual achievement of our species. Culture is the art, faiths, customs, and social institutions of a given people at a given time. Clark tells the tale of a culture that has been all but lost to the horrors of war. In "The

Portable Phonograph" Walter Van Tilburg Clark uses dialogue, setting, and symbolism to illustrate how easily humanity's art, beliefs, and institutions can slip away as mankind reverts to its natural state of savagery and war.

### Questions To Ask

- Is the main idea of the essay clearly stated in the introduction and then reinforced in the thesis? Have you provided a "hook" to seize your reader's attention and persuade her to continue reading? After reading only the introduction, does your reader have a clear idea of what the essay will cover?
- Have you written a strong thesis statement and included it as the last sentence of your introductory paragraph?

# Hook

Effective essays often begin with some type of hook to get the reader's attention. The hook is appropriately named, for it is just like a fish hook. Its function is to catch the reader. A good hook is something that entices the reader or wets his curiosity in some way. Ask yourself what you can say that is so interesting or provocative that a someone will put everything else in her life on hold in order to read your essay. There are countless ways to hook your reader, but a few of the most common methods are as follows:

1. Use an anecdote from your own experience (for narrative essays).
2. Explain an interesting but little-known fact.
3. Cite a shocking or provocative statistic.
4. Begin with a highly effective image.
5. Find common ground with the reader; appeal to universal human concerns.
6. Make a shocking statement or proposal.
7. Address a hot-button issue in a new and surprising way.
8. Relate your topic to another well-known case.

### Do

- Come up with a powerful and imaginative way to begin your essay. Be provocative or shocking.
- Appeal to your reader's insecurities, hopes, dreams, and fears. Share a personal experience.

### Do Not

- Do not begin with a quotation. If you do use a quotation in your first sentence, that quotation should be woven into your own language. The first character of your essay should never be a quotation mark.
- Do not be aggressive, insulting, or offensive. Do not begin with a cliche.

- Do not begin with a rhetorical question.
- Do not write anything in your hook that does not logically anticipate your essay's broader argument.

## Examples

It has been observed, that a dwarf standing on the shoulders of a giant will see farther than the giant himself; and the moderns, standing as they do on the vantage ground of former discoveries, and uniting all the fruits of the experience of their forefathers with their own actual observation, may be admitted to enjoy a more enlarged and comprehensive view of things than the ancients themselves; for that alone is true antiquity, which embraces the antiquity of the world, and not that which would refer us back to a period when the world was young. **- Charles Colton**

When I look back over the years I see myself, a little child of scarcely four years of age, walking in front of my nurse, in a green English lane, and listening to her tell another of her kind that my mother is Chinese. "Oh Lord!" exclaims the informed. She turns around and scans me curiously from head to foot. Then the two women whisper together. Tho the word "Chinese" conveys very little meaning to my mind, I feel that they are talking about my father and mother and my heart swells with indignation. When we reach home I rush to my mother and try to tell her what I have heard.
I am a young child. I fail to make myself intelligible. My mother does not understand, and when the nurse declares to her, "Little Miss Sui is a story-teller," my mother slaps me. **- Sui Sin Far**

In English writing we seldom speak of tradition, though we occasionally apply its name in deploring its absence. We cannot refer to ";the tradition" or to "a tradition"; at most, we employ the adjective in saying that the poetry of So-and-so is "traditional" or even "too traditional." Seldom, perhaps, does the word appear except in a phrase of censure. If otherwise, it is vaguely approbative, with the implication, as to the work approved, of some pleasing archeological reconstruction. You can hardly make the word agreeable to English ears without this comfortable reference to the reassuring science of archeology.
**- T. S. Eliot**

The vast streams of this Western Continent flowed over a nameless course during that mysterious past whose secrets we would so gladly unveil. There are rivers on the globe, like the Jordan, the Euphrates, the Nile, the Tiber, which are known to have borne during thousands of years the names they bear to-day. But this Western hemisphere, shrouded in mystery, has no

primeval names to repeat to us for the noble streams flowing from its heart.
- **Susan Fenimore Cooper**

Some years ago, in company with an agreeable party, I spent a long summer day in exploring the Mammoth Cave in Kentucky. We traversed, through spacious galleries affording a solid masonry foundation for the town and county overhead, the six or eight black miles from the mouth of the cavern to the innermost recess which tourists visit, a niche or grotto made of one seamless stalactite, and called, I believe, Serena"s Bower. I lost the light of one day. I saw high domes, and bottomless pits; heard the voice of unseen waterfalls; paddled three quarters of a mile in the deep Echo River, whose waters are peopled with the blind fish; crossed the streams "Lethe" and "Styx;" plied with music and guns the echoes in these alarming galleries; saw every form of stalagmite and stalactite in the sculptured and fretted chambers,--icicle, orange-flower, acanthus, grapes, and snowball. We shot Bengal lights into the vaults and groins of the sparry cathedrals, and examined all the masterpieces which the four combined engineers, water, limestone, gravitation, and time, could make in the dark. The mysteries and scenery of the cave had the same dignity that belongs to all natural objects, and which shames the fine things to which we foppishly compare them. - **Ralph Waldo Emerson**

## Questions To Ask
- Have you employed a clever tactic to seize your reader's attention?
- Is your hook appropriate to your topic?
- Is your hook a non sequitur?
- Have you avoided cliches, rhetorical questions, and long (or full) quotations?

# Thesis

A thesis is an explicit, comprehensive, and all-controlling statement that clearly articulates what an entire essay will be about. The thesis statement should be the last sentence in an essay's introductory paragraph and should still make sense and function well if removed from the essay and read in isolation. An essay should not cover any material or develop any ideas that are not presented or implied in the thesis. The thesis statement is the most important sentence in any essay. More time should be spent writing, revising, and editing the thesis than any other sentence in the paper. A good thesis statement should be exceptionally specific, clear, fluent, well-worded, and comprehensive yet as concise as possible without degrading the overall sentence.

**Do**

- Position your thesis as the last sentence of your introductory paragraph.
- Write in active voice with strong verbs, specific concrete nouns, and well-placed adjectives and adverbs that appropriately clarify or further define the topic at hand.
- Restate any needed information such as authors' names, titles of works, locations, studies, laws, entities, etc. that are associated with the topic. Test this by removing your thesis from the introductory paragraph and reading it in isolation. Is the topic of the essay still explicitly clear?
- If you are responding to a prompt, consider using key phrases from the prompt in your thesis. This will focus your essay, signal on-topic writing, and aid you in your efforts to narrow your topic to a manageable scope
- Limit your thesis to one sentence.

**Do Not**

- Do not use pronouns or indefinite identifiers in your thesis. Avoid words and phrases like "this," "that law," "the author," "he," "they," "this problem," etc.
- Do not include quotations or any other non-essential details in your thesis. Usually, the thesis statement should be limited to your own original words and thoughts.
- Do not attempt to use a question as your thesis. A thesis is a statement, not a question. Explicitly tell the reader what your paper will cover. Do not rely upon the reader to guess or infer.
- Do not be too wordy or long-winded in your thesis. A good thesis statement runs between fifteen and thirty-five words long.

**Examples**

- In *The Great Gatsby* F. Scott Fitzgerald uses well-developed characters, vivid imagery, and archetypal symbolism to explore the human tendency to take one's current position for granted and live so far in the future that it becomes impossible to be happy in the present.
- By withholding crucial exposition, using a complex and highly developed conflict, and vividly illustrating the intricate nuances of Native American culture, Tom Whitecloud accurately portrays a young Indian's internal struggle to find his place within contemporary American society.
- Frances Perkins was responsible for the early social reformation of New York City, and later as the United States Secretary of Labor, she played a large role in the drafting and implementation of The New Deal.

**Questions To Ask**

- Does your thesis still make sense if you remove it from the introductory paragraph and read it in isolation?
- In your thesis, do you clearly restate the issue at hand and the several sub-points you will make to prove your point?
- Is your thesis wordy, long-winded, or hard to follow?
- After you finished writing your paper, did you return to your thesis and make sure it is still sufficient?

# Paragraphing

The body paragraphs of an essay should be intentionally structured for maximum clarity, completeness, specificity, and rhetorical strength. Each paragraph should begin with a strong topic sentence and should develop only one idea (see "Topic Sentences" within this guide). A topic sentence should prove or develop one aspect of the assertion made in the thesis statement. Likewise, the sentences in a paragraph should prove or develop the point made in its topic sentence. Any writing that does not help to prove or develop the idea that is presented in that paragraph's topic sentence is extraneous and should be deleted or examined in a dedicated paragraph of its own.

In order to prove the point made in a topic sentence (or develop the idea found there), a writer must collect objective evidence about the issue (facts, quotations, statistics, etc.), present that evidence to the reader, and provide analysis that explains how the evidence presented proves the point made in the topic sentence. A writer should think of himself like a trial lawyer who is attempting to prove a point before a jury in court. A theory must be proposed, evidence must be gathered and presented, and an argument must be made to show how that evidence proves that his client is not guilty. In the case of writing an essay, the thesis is like an overall plea of "Not Guilty"; the topic sentences are like DNA evidence, alibi evidence, eye-whiteness testimony, etc.; and the sentences in each paragraph are like his arguments before the jury.

**Paragraph Development -** The assertion made in a paragraph's topic sentence must be supported with ample evidence, argument, and analysis. Paragraphs that are not fully developed lack persuasive strength and are not usually fully convincing. In order to develop a paragraph, a writer must use evidence, analysis, and commentary to develop or prove the point she makes in her topic sentence. In turn, each topic sentence develops or proves the point she makes in her thesis. Short paragraphs are rarely well developed. Generally, a paragraph must contain at least four sentences in order to approach anything resembling full development.

**Evidence (EV) -** Evidence is the small bits of objective data a writer uses in order to develop or prove the assertion made in a paragraph's topic sentence. Evidence is essential to the overall effectiveness of a paragraph, for without these objective details, a paragraph is like a trial without evidence, just theory and conjecture. A piece of evidence is any objective (i.e. verifiable) bit of information that helps prove the point made in the topic sentence. A few of the most common types of evidence are as follows:

- Quotations
- Facts
- Examples
- Details
- Statistics
- Expert testimony

*°Most effective paragraphs contain at least two pieces of evidence.°*

**Analysis (AN) -** Analysis is a general term used to describe any original remarks made by a writer within a paragraph to explain or prove a point. In order to write an effective paragraph, a writer must make an assertion (the topic sentence), back up that assertion with evidence (quotations, facts, statistics, etc.), and then explain how the evidence presented proves the original assertion she made in her topic sentence. The overall effectiveness of an essay often rests upon the strength of its analysis. An essay that lacks adequate analysis is like a trial where the jury is left to analyze the evidence on their own without hearing the defense or prosecution lawyers make their cases. Analysis can take many forms, but a few of the most common types are as follows:

- Logical, ethical, and emotional appeals
- Explanatory or clarifying remarks
- Argument
- Description
- Definition
- Synthesis (connecting scattered elements to form a whole)

*°°Most effective paragraphs employ at least two well-written analytical sentences to support every piece of evidence.°°*

**Paragraph Format -** Many writers find it useful to use a paragraph template. This technique can be very effective. However, if you use a paragraph template, your goal should be to disguise that fact at all costs. The fluency and flow of your writing should prevent readers from recognizing a formula or pattern to your paragraphs. One popular paragraph pattern is as follows:

**TS - (Topic Sentence) -** An explicit controlling statement that explains exactly what the entire paragraph will be about.

**CM - (Commentary) -** A lead-in or opening remark that introduces the first piece of evidence.

**EV - (Evidence) -** The first piece of objective evidence that helps develop or prove the assertion made in the topic sentence.

**AN -** A writer's original comments (argument, analysis, persuasive appeals, synthesis, etc.) that explain how the first piece of evidence proves or supports the assertion made in the topic sentence.

**EV -** The second piece of objective evidence that helps develop or prove the assertion made in the topic sentence.

**AN -** A writer's original comments (argument, analysis, persuasive appeals, synthesis, etc.) that explain how the second piece of evidence proves or supports the assertion made in the topic sentence.

*\* For a illustrated example of a well-developed paragraph, see "Paragraph Development" within this guide.\**

*\*\*Whenever possible, quotations should be woven into the natural flow of a writer's prose. For quote weaving, see "Quotations" within this guide.\*\**

## Patterns of Development

1. **Description -** Examines the specific details of a subject in order to fully depict and explain it.
2. **Illustration -** Uses one or more specific examples to prove a point.
3. **Cause and Effect -** Evaluates the causal relationships at play within a given subject.
4. **Comparison and Contrast -** Analyzes the similarities and differences of two or more topics.
5. **Classification and Division -** Breaks a subject down into its elemental parts and examines the nature of those parts.
6. **Problem and Solution -** Scrutinizes a given issue and proposes a resolution.
7. **Analogy -** Compares a given subject to another unrelated and more widely known subject.

8.  **Definition** - Extends the definition of a term in order to fully explain an idea or concept.
9.  **Narration** - Tells a story in order to develop an overall main idea.

**Do**

- Develop your paragraphs with specific evidence.
- Use at least two pieces of evidence in every paragraph.
- Provide ample commentary, argument, and analysis to prove why the evidence you have included proves or develops the idea you assert in your topic sentence.

**Do Not**

- Do not write paragraphs shorter than four sentences.
- Do not include long quotations within your paragraph.
- Weave your quotations into the natural flow of your sentences.
- Do not begin a paragraph with a question or a quote.
- Do not include anything in a paragraph that does not directly support its topic sentence.

**Examples**

Modern writers hoped to break free from the old paradigms of writing. They began to experiment with new forms of mechanics, syntax, usage and grammar. Some, like Gertrude Stein, even hoped to create the literary equivalent of Picasso's Cubism, thus removing any imbedded meaning from the text. By doing so, they helped to usher in an entirely new literary theory called Reader Response, which supports the claim the there is no one correct reading of a text; rather, each reader determines his or her meaning. **[This paragraph is a bit too short and lacks full development.]**

Ernest Hemingway forever changed the literature of the English language with his unique style of prose. Hemingway uses short, choppy sentences that leave the reader to do all the work. The crown prince of simple sentences, Hemingway's prose style brings his stories to life by evoking vivid imagery in the mind of the reader. In "The Big Two-Hearted River," Hemingway tells a characteristic tale of a fisherman's unity with nature. He writes, "Nick looked down into the pool from the bridge. It was a hot day" (Hemingway 1340). Terse sentences such as these create a sense of brevity and blunt directness, but they also strangely reveal--as the famous analogy goes--the larger part of the Hemingway iceberg looming just beneath the surface. Hemingway goes on to write, "a big trout shot upstream in a long angle, only his shadow marking the angle, then lost his shadow as he came back through the surface of the water, caught the sun, and then . . . went back into the stream under the surface"

(1341). Hemingway's unique Modern style becomes evident from highly pointed yet strangely colorful sentences such as this. By including only what is essential, Hemingway allows the reader's mind to fill in the gaps--a truly Modern idea.

The recent study titled "ADD and Reading Disability" has proven that Attention Deficit Disorder (ADD) is linked to and often causes Reading Disability (RD). Preformed by the University of Houston, this important study has shown that "the presence of ADD is associated with a general reduction of performance across tasks and groups" (Breier 238). Researchers analyzed the psychoacoustic responses of 150 carefully selected children in order to measure auditory temporal activity and binaural temporal function (i.e. brain functions that also relate to reading). The study was performed under the hypothesis that children with ADD and RD would exhibit deficits on these psychoacoustic tasks, and the study would therefore show that ADD and RD are linked and cause significant reading difficulties (Breier 233). The results of the study were conclusive and alarming. The research showed that the presence of ADD is a significant factor that negatively affects a child's ability to read. But, even more alarmingly, it showed that dyslexia (RD) and ADD interact synergistically. Therefore, ADD, which causes a reader's mind to wonder away from the text, interacts with and often hints at the presence of RD, a disorder which prevents a reader from effectively decoding written text (Breier 240). Thus, this seminal study proves ADD to be a major cause of reading difficulty.

It is evident that online privacy remains a major issue within the United States Congress. However, identifying a problem and finding its solutions are two different things. Within the last several years, Internet use has more than doubled, yet the online privacy debate has only recently emerged as a primary issue within internet-related legislation. Many of these issues were raised in previous bills, but they only survived long enough to be introduced and briefly debated. Now, as Congress members have begun to take online privacy more seriously, they are resurrecting many of those old discarded issues and examining them with greater scrutiny and a more heightened sense of urgency. In consequence, there is a very good chance that in the coming years Congress will pass a large number of Internet privacy laws. Many Internet privacy issues have already been brought to the floor and debated, and with Congress's new motivation to act, these important bills will most likely be fast-tracked through the system and very quickly become law.

**Questions To Ask**

- If you were to present your paragraph to a jury, would you have included enough evidence to be fully convincing?
- Does your paragraph begin with an idea in the topic sentence and then prove that idea with objective evidence and scholarly analysis?
- Have you presented more than one idea in your paragraph? Limit each paragraph to the development of one idea.
- Have you introduced and explained each quotation and bit of evidence that you include?

# Topic Sentences

The first sentence of every paragraph is its topic sentence. A topic sentence is an explicit controlling statement that explains exactly what the entire paragraph will be about.

## Factors To Consider

- Every topic sentence must directly relate to the essay's thesis statement by proving or developing one aspect of the assertion or point made within that thesis.
- All content within a paragraph should directly support the point or assertion made in the topic sentence. Any writing that does not directly support a paragraph's topic sentence should be deleted or examined in a paragraph of its own.
- Topic sentences should be exceptionally clear, direct, and well written.
- A reader should be able to understand an essay's general topic, argument, and meaning after reading only its thesis and the first sentence of every paragraph (topic sentences).
- Think of topic sentences as the main points of your argument. For example, if your thesis asserts that the death penalty is unconstitutional, your topic sentences will state the several reasons why.

## Do

- Use topic sentence to support your thesis. Topic sentences should explain or develop one aspect of the idea you asserted in your thesis statement.
- Place your topic sentence at the beginning of every paragraph, the first sentence. Use your topic sentence to directly state what that paragraph will cover.

### Do Not

- Do not begin a paragraph with a question or a quotation.
- Do not bury your topic sentence in the middle of a paragraph.
- Do not lead up to your topic sentence at the end of a paragraph.
- Do not write topic sentences that fail to directly support your essay's thesis statement.

### Examples

- Congress is now considering tough new internet privacy laws in order to protect consumers who want to feel safe about using their computers at home to conduct business and shop online.
- With the goal of offering fifth generation (5G) services before 2012, wireless companies are currently scrambling to develop new technologies for mobile devices and the wireless web.
- In order to increase profits and help curb the rising cost of medical insurance in the United States, private companies are now collecting and archiving the personal medical information of American citizens without those patients' knowledge or consent.
- Attention Deficit/Hyperactivity Disorder (ADD) is the most common childhood psychiatric condition in the Unites States today.

# Quotations

Quoting the words of others is a very powerful technique in essay writing. However, when done improperly, quotations can hinder an essay rather than help it. Quotations are best used as evidence (i.e. objective data that prove the assertion made in a topic sentence). Use quotations as evidence to support the claim you make in your topic sentence, which in turn supports your thesis sentence.

### Do

- All quotations should be introduced and fully explained with scholarly analysis; this is one reason why a paragraph or an essay should never begin with a quotation.
- Do not leave anything to the reader's imagination. Make sure to lead into a quotation in order to get your reader ready for it, and then make sure to fully explain why those words prove the issue at hand.
- Weave small chunks of a larger quotation into the natural flow of your writing (see examples below).
- Cite all quotations with MLA or APA as required.
- Credit the speaker of the quotation. Never leave your reader to guess whose words you are quoting.

# Do Not

- Do not write long quotations. These foreign objects often disrupt the rhetorical and linguistic flow of a writer's paragraphs and overall essay.
- Do not misquote the original source. The quotation must be copied exactly as it is. Retain all punctuation and formatting such as italics and bolding.

## Examples

The tone of "Sonnet 129" is one of disgust, for words like "waste," "shame," "murderous," "rude," and "despised" make the reader feel as if he or she is being scolded.

In "Afloat in Thick Deeps: Shakespeare's Sonnets on Certainty," Engle argues that Shakespeare's sonnets explore a "de-idealized, or anti-Platonic," notion of how things hang together: a world view in which "truth" and lasting value are simply what a "mutable community" chooses to regard as "good for a long time" (832).

Sarah blames everyone but herself for her decision to leave school and discounts education as "useless." As her support systems crumble one after another, she says that she used to be a Christian like her friends, but now she is sure that "there is no God."

This haughty tone can be seen, for example, in the writing of the Countess of Dia who extols her own "beauty, virtue, and intelligence" (Bogin 85) and who makes the following statement: "My worth and my noble birth should have some weight, / my beauty and especially my noble thoughts" (87).

## Questions To Ask

- Does your use of quotations detract from the clarity and flow of the essay?
- Have you woven your quotations into the natural flow of your own writing?
- Have you gotten every quotation exactly right, retaining even the italics and punctuation that exists in the original quotation?
- Do the quotations you have chosen actually prove the point you are trying to make? Or are they off-topic and random?
- Have you made sure to credit the speaker of each individual quotation? This can be done with a signal phrase or a parenthetical citation.
- Have you introduced and explained each and every quotation? Do not drop quotations on your reader without warning.
- Have you refrained from the use of long quotations, which generally disrupt the rhetorical and aesthetic coherence of an essay?

# Transitions

Use transitions both within and among paragraphs in order to provide clear connections between ideas, signal new thoughts, and separate sections of text. Appropriate use of transitional words and phrases helps readers follow the flow of arguments within an essay and bolsters its rhetorical strength.

## Transitional Words and Phrases

1. **Illustration** - thus, for example, for instance, namely, to illustrate, in other words, in particular, specifically, such as.
2. **Contrast** - on the contrary, contrarily, notwithstanding, but, however, nevertheless, in spite of, in contrast, yet, on one hand, on the other hand, rather, or, nor, conversely, at the same time, while this may be true.
3. **Addition** - and, in addition to, furthermore, moreover, besides, than, too, also, both-and, another, equally important, first, second, etc., again, further, last, finally, not only-but also, as well as, in the second place, next, likewise, similarly, in fact, as a result, consequently, in the same way, for example, for instance, however, thus, therefore, otherwise.
4. **Time** - after, afterward, before, then, once, next, last, at last, at length, first, second, etc., at first, formerly, rarely, usually, another, finally, soon, meanwhile, at the same time, for a minute, hour, day, etc., during the morning, day, week, etc., most important, later, ordinarily, to begin with, afterwards, generally, in order to, subsequently, previously, in the meantime, immediately, eventually, concurrently, simultaneously.
5. **Space** - at the left, at the right, in the center, on the side, along the edge, on top, below, beneath, under, around, above, over, straight ahead, at the top, at the bottom, surrounding, opposite, at the rear, at the front, in front of, beside, behind, next to, nearby, in the distance, beyond, in the forefront, in the foreground, within sight, out of sight, across, under, nearer, adjacent, in the background.
6. **Concession** - although, at any rate, at least, still, thought, even though, granted that, while it may be true, in spite of, of course.
7. **Similarity or Comparison** - similarly, likewise, in like fashion, in like manner, analogous to.
8. **Emphasis** - above all, indeed, truly, of course, certainly, surely, in fact, really, in truth, again, besides, also, furthermore, in addition.
9. **Details** - specifically, especially, in particular, to explain, to list, to enumerate, in detail, namely, including.

10. **Examples** - for example, for instance, to illustrate, thus, in other words, as an illustration, in particular.
11. **Consequence or Result** - so that, with the result that, thus, consequently, hence, accordingly, for this reason, therefore, so, because, since, due to, as a result, in other words, then..
12. **Summary** - therefore, finally, consequently, thus, in short, in conclusion, in brief, as a result, accordingly.
13. **Suggestion** - for this purpose, to this end, with this in mind, with this purpose in mind, therefore.

## Do

- Use transition words both within and among paragraphs. Use transition words to signal new or contradictory ideas.
- Use transition words to help clarify complex arguments and ideas.

## Do Not

- Do not use so many transitions that they disrupt the flow of your paper. Do not use the wrong type of transition for the intended purpose.
- Do not use transitions that conflict with the established style of your paper.

## Examples

- Consequently, consumers now feel safer about using their computers at work to conduct business and shop online.
- Accordingly, Billy Pilgrim has adjusted his own sight to conform to his new alien surroundings.
- Some believe that Global warming is a myth; however, some also believe that the United States faked the moon landings.
- Attention Deficit/Hyperactivity Disorder (ADD) is the most common childhood psychiatric condition in the United States today. In fact, three out of ten children in the United States are currently diagnosed with ADD.

## Questions To Ask

- Do the transitions you employ enhance the fluency and flow of your writing, or do they make your writing more difficult to follow?
- Have you used transitions to clarify long sentences and complex ideas?
- Are you sure you understand the transitions you have used and have employed them correctly.
- Have you used transitions to control the flow of your paragraphs as well as the content within those paragraphs?

# Conclusion

Tie your essay together by revisiting the central points that you have made. Wrap up your argument by restating the idea you asserted in your thesis (although in different words). Reiterate several of your most important points as evidence that you have proven or fully developed the idea you originally asserted in your thesis. Then, leave your reader with something interesting to consider. Remember, this is your last chance to impress your reader and, most likely, the last thing she will remember.

### Do

- Work on including a powerful and imaginative way to end your essay.
- Keep in mind that this is the last thing the reader (and grader) will read and remember.
- Recap the main elements of your essay and drive your point home.
- Try to leave the reader with something to think about--some little nugget of wisdom that ties everything together.
- A few things you might consider doing in your conclusion are as follows:
  - Summarize your main points.
  - Ask a stimulating question.
  - Employ one final quotation.
  - Call your reader to action.
  - Relate the issue to our world today.
  - End with vivid imagery.
  - Suggest a solution.
  - End with an ominous warning.

### Do Not

- Do not introduce any new ideas or arguments in your conclusion.
- Do not be wordy or long-winded.
- Do not be overly dramatic.
- Do not try to rehash every fine detail of your argument.
- Do not apologize.
- Do not restate your thesis word-for-word.

### Examples

William Butler Yeats would found literature on three basic tenets: freedom, God, and immortality. In doing so, he champions the very philosophy Immanuel Kant debunks in his philosophical inquiry into human reason, that one cannot know any truth beyond his or her own sensory perceptions and the internal a priori framework holding them together. But due to the power of literary symbolism, Yeats believed the opposite to be true, and he based his entire poetic craft upon that notion. Namely--as evidenced by his journals, letters, and the overall body of his work--Yeats believed that literature, above all things, allows human beings to transcend rational thought and acquire truths that are wholly unattainable by any other means. Thus, for Yeats, literary symbolism becomes mystically powerful and transmits the clearest and most important of all messages. Resting upon the foundation of freedom, God, and immortality, literary symbolism transmits universal truth.


So I do not think that it is altogether fanciful or incredible to suppose that even the floods in London may be accepted and enjoyed poetically. Nothing beyond inconvenience seems really to have been caused by them; and inconvenience, as I have said, is only one aspect, and that the most unimaginative and accidental aspect of a really romantic situation. An adventure is only an inconvenience rightly considered. An inconvenience is only an adventure wrongly considered. The water that girdled the houses and shops of London must, if anything, have only increased their previous witchery and wonder. For as the Roman Catholic priest in the story said - "Wine is good with everything except water," and on a similar principle, water is good with everything except wine. **- G. H. Chesterton**


Jane Adams's contributions to the United States are countless, but in the span of her life she crusaded for such causes as progressive education, child labor legislation, housing reform, criminology, fair immigrant treatment, organized labor, direct democracy, feminism, and pacifism. Mrs. Adams's actions gave support to her philosophies and character to her words. As the driving force behind the United States transition from a rural agricultural nation to an urban industrial powerhouse, she changed and molded the country like few others before or after. Though history seems to have forgotten Mrs. Adams, her contributions can never be totally overlooked, for in our society today her legacy is evident to anyone who takes a moment to look. Jane Adams was one of those rare individuals who was crazy enough to think that she could change the world. She just happened to be right.


In conclusion, there are many positive and negative effects of space exploration. Large-scale space exploration is likely to have a temporary negative effect on humanity due to an increased probability for large catastrophes and higher taxes. But these disadvantages are greatly outweighed by the potential benefits of exploring space. Future missions will bolster industries across the globe, create countless new jobs and enterprises, and enhance education worldwide. Although some might disagree with spending taxpayer money to explore the universe, the untold number of life-changing advancements and discoveries space exploration is sure to yield will one day prove those dollars to have been well spent.

In conclusion, global warming is a real, scientifically proven, man-made phenomenon that is currently affecting our world in many horrendous ways. The world's climate stands at the precipice of a continual pattern of logarithmically accelerating global warming. This radical change in our planet's climate is a man-made phenomenon caused by large-scale deforestation and the burning of fossil fuels. These human activities cause increased levels of carbon dioxide, ozone gasses, and water vapor in the atmosphere, which leads to global warming. Without immediate and drastic changes to the laws that govern emissions, logging, and agriculture, the planet Earth will continue to experience run- away greenhouse warming due to the greed and negligence of the human race.

## Questions To Ask

- Have you reasserted the idea you present in your thesis, summed up your key arguments, and left your reader with something interesting to think about?
- Have you expanded the content of your analysis without presenting new ideas?
- Have you tied the many wide-ranging ideas and arguments of your essay into one tidy package?
- Have you provided a different context for (or new way of looking at) your argument?
- Have you recommended a solution or called your reader to action?

# Other Punctuation

## Dash
Use a dash to set off a parenthetical element (i.e. an interrupting thought). A dash is two hyphens joining two words with no spaces--like this.
- If you open a dash, you must close it (just like parentheses).
- If the parenthetical expression ends the sentence, the closing dash is not required.

## Examples
- Paradigms are solid--well built for some but impenetrable for most.
- For these we require a shift in paradigm. Shifts of this sort--changes in the fundamental assumptions we use to describe our worlds--can only be achieved through extreme trauma or overwhelming resolve.

## Ellipsis
Use an ellipsis to show that you have removed a portion of text. Ellipses show omission. An ellipsis consists of four spaces and three periods, like this_._._._
- When omitting full sentences from a quotation, the ellipsis goes after the period in the last sentence before the omission.
- Be mindful that many word processing programs insert special characters for ellipses. Those special characters are not actually true and correct ellipses.

## Examples
- Herman Melville warns his readers, "Look not too long in the face of the fire. O man! Never dream with thy hand on the helm. . . . Believe not the artificial fire when its redness makes all things look ghastly."
- Theodore Roosevelt proclaims that "The best executive is one who has . . . self-restraint enough to keep from meddling with [her employees while they work]."
- Abraham Lincoln is famous for saying, "I am not bound to win . . . but I am bound to live by the light that I have."

# Comma

## Introductory Elements
Use a comma after an introductory word, phrase, or clause.

## Examples
- Although it is raining outside, we are still going to have practice today.
- In order for you to be fully prepared for the test, get out your *Huck Finn* books and study chapter seventeen.
- If you touch the muffler, you will burn your leg.
- Instead of just complaining, get up and do something about the situation.
- However hard you try, you will never change my mind.
- Around the side of the house on the porch, you will find my screwdriver.
- Whether we like it or not, it is still eighty-five degrees in November.
- Because we are so awesome, we are going to ace the SAT.
- Besides the fact that my desk is falling apart, this classroom is fine.
- Frankly, I think Snoop Dog is wonderful.
- In 1945 many Native Americans fought in WWII. (With only one prepositional phrase, the comma is optional)

## Words and Phrases That Signal an Introductory Element
- after, although
- in as much as, as if, as though, because
- before
- even if, even though, if
- in order that, providing that, provided that, now that, once
- seeing as how, seeing that, since
- so, so that, though, unless, until
- when, whereas, wherever
- no matter where, when, why, etc., whenever
- however, whichever, whoever, whosoever, whatever

## Compound Sentences
Use a comma and a coordinating conjunction (IC, cc IC) to join two full sentences (independent clauses - IC). Failure to use a comma after the coordinating conjunction in a compound sentence results in a run-on sentence. To identify a compound sentence, look for two complete thoughts. Usually, if there is a second subject after a coordinating conjunction, it is a compound sentence and needs a comma before the coordinating conjunction:  **and, or, nor, for, but, yet, so.**

**Examples**
- Mr. Green's Toyota Yaris is a fly ride with spinners, and he is going to get hydraulics in the spring.
- The jet-black caprice arrived on the scene, and Detective Smith stepped out from the passenger's side.
- During Homer's wedding, he lit the unity candle, but he accidentally caught Mary's glove on fire.
- Everybody knows that two plus two is five, yet a few of you still think two plus two is four.
- The electroshock therapy treatments are working well, but I still have a long way to go.
- Some have said that Eminem is a lyrical genius, but I am fairly certain that he is an extraterrestrial time traveler from another dimension.
- I am missing my right eye, and my left one is not any good.
- The weather man said it would be cool today, yet the cold front has not yet arrived.
- Joe jumped off of the tallest cliff at Pace Bend Park, and the wind swept him to the left, but he did not get hurt.
- Bob Dylan said he always thought he was a "song and dance man," but he is truly a poet.
- He hit the ball, and he ran the bases.
- He hit the ball and ran the bases. (No second subject = No comma)

## Non-Restrictive Elements

Use commas to enclose non-restrictive (i.e. non-essential) portions of a sentence. A non-restrictive element is a word, phrase, or dependent clause within a sentence that does not restrict (i.e. change) the meaning of the sentence. Think of non-restrictive elements as added stuff, for they do not change the meaning of the sentence and must be isolated with commas. Restrictive elements go without commas.

## How To Identify Non-Restrictive Elements
- It is not essential to the sentence.
- It can be deleted without changing the sentence's basic meaning
- The words *that* and *because* always set up restrictive elements and should never have commas before them.
- The word *which* always sets up a restrictive element and should always have a comma before it.
- As an indication that it is not essential, a non-restrictive element is always set off from the rest of the sentence with commas.

## Examples
- Bosephus, a slightly plump older man, was never quite able to escape the weird looks people would give him.
- Sally is really into falconry, a sport that has grown in recent years.
- Beef a popular flavor of Ramen Noodles has been discontinued.
- Beef Ramen Noodles, a popular flavor, has been discontinued.
- Ms. Smith planned the test for December 7th, which is also Sam's birthday.
- Some who are more familiar with the works of Mark Twain have considered this point.
- The shirt, after all, was pink with yellow polka dots.
- Today's club meeting, I am sorry to say, has been cancelled.
- Mr. Carver, for example, was here for eight years.
- The novel takes place in China, where many languages are spoken.
- The novel takes place in a land where many languages are spoken.
- Mrs. Green, our teacher, is an awesome person.
- The teacher Mrs. Green is an awesome person.

## Items in Series
Use commas to set off all items in a series, **even the last one.**

## Examples
- I like apples, oranges, and pears.
- I like guns and ammo, books and movies, and unicorns and glitter.
- He was tall, dark, and handsome.
- Favio, George, and William will be in the play.

## Transitional and Interrupting Expressions
Use commas to set off transitional expressions, contrasting elements, interjections, direct address, and ending questions.

## Examples
- Longhorn fans, moreover, have far more spirit than anyone else. (Transitional Expression)
- He did not tie down his load, did he? (Ending Question)
- I repeat it, sir, we must fight. (Direct Address)
- What do you think, Mr. President? (Direct Address)
- Dear Lord, she was the fastest swimmer I had ever seen. (Interjection)
- It was Darth Vader, not Luke, who brought balance back to the force. (Contrasting Element)

### Dates and Addresses

Use commas to set off days, months, years, cities, and states.

### Examples

- I am sure that Austin, Texas, was the address on the card.
- The expression 9/11 refers to the terrorist attacks on September 11, 2001, in Manhattan, New York, and elsewhere around the nation.

### Quotations and Dialogue

Use commas to signal dialogue and quotations. **Do not use a comma where the a quotation seems to start with that.**

### Examples

- A very wise saying warns, "Never treat anyone the way you wouldn't want to be treated."
- "I don't want," Henry said, "to get to the end of my life only to find out I haven't lived."
- Who said "She is very beautiful"?
- Sally insisted that I "will never win the race."

# Apostrophe

### Possession

Use an apostrophe to show possession. For plural words that end with the letter *s*, place the apostrophe after the last letter of the word (e.g. students').

### Examples

- Sally's stack of books is bigger than hers.
- Bill Gates's wealth is valued somewhere around fifty billion.
- Chris's glasses are broken.
- The rifle's barrel needs to be cleaned.
- The student's car was totalled.
- The students' teacher was absent today.
- The difference between Sally William's and Hailey Buckner's projects is easy to see.

### Contractions

Use an apostrophe to show omission of letters in contractions.

### Examples

- it's = it is

- wasn't = was not
- don't = do not
- they're = they are
- who's = who is (not whose)
- can't = cannot

# Quotation Marks

### Punctuation Rules
In standard American English, commas and periods go inside quotation marks. All other punctuation marks go outside unless retained from the original quotation.

### Examples
- "Indeed," said Mr. Utterson with a slight change of tone, "and what was her request?" "The ages are all equal," says William Blake, "but genius is always above its age." What is it that we are now calling "fundamentalism"?
- Edgar asked, "What is fundamentalism?"
- The title of Colin Shanafelt's story is "What Gods Would Be Theirs?" Do not allow yourselves to be "betrayed with a kiss"!
- "She is really 'cute,'" William said, "but I'm not looking for another romance." (a quote within a quote) I had the following emotions after reading the essay "Self-Reliance": sorrow, fear, hope, and longing. "Run!" a man exclaimed from the second floor.

### Titles
Enclose the titles of short works in quotation marks. Ask yourself if the piece is part of a larger work (i.e. part of a whole); if so, enclose its title in quotation marks.

### Types of Works To Write in Quotations
- songs, poems, short stories, essays
- magazine articles, journal articles, book chapters, pages from a website
- works from an anthology

### Examples
- My favorite song is "Stairway To Heaven."
- "The Try-Works" is my favorite chapter of *Moby-Dick*.
- "The Singularity Approaches" is an influential article that appeared in *Time Magazine*.
- *CNN.com* ran a story entitled "Education: Why It Matters."

## Direct Quotations

Use quotation marks to signal a direct quotation. Use single quotation marks (i.e. apostrophe) to set off quotations within quotations.

### Examples

- It has been said that "common souls pay with what they do, nobler souls with that which they are."
- Ralph Waldo Emerson writes, "It has been said that 'common souls pay with what they do, nobler souls with that which they are.'"
- The nightingale remarks, "For Love his servant evermore ammendeth."
- Indeed one might ask, as a physician: "How did such a malady attack that finest product of antiquity, Plato?"
- The tone of "Sonnet 129" is one of disgust, for words like "waste," "shame," "murderous," "rude," and "despised" make the reader feel as if he or she is being scolded.
- Sally said, "The sky looks beautiful today."

## Long Quotations

Quotations that run more than four typed lines should be set apart from the main text of the essay and indented one inch from the left margin. No quotation marks are necessary, unless they are retained from the original quotation.

### Example

> But now when it has been surmounted, when Europe, rid of this nightmare, can again draw breath freely and at least enjoy a healthier sleep, we, WHOSE DUTY IS WAKEFULNESS ITSELF, are the heirs of all the strength which the struggle against this error has fostered. It amounted to the very inversion of truth, and the denial of the PERSPECTIVE--"the fundamental condition"of life, to speak of Spirit and the Good as Plato spoke of them; indeed one might ask, as a physician: "How did such a malady attack that finest product of antiquity, Plato? Had the wicked Socrates really corrupted him? Was Socrates after all a corrupter of youths, and deserved his hemlock?" (Nietzsche 145)

## Poetry

Quote lines of poetry with quotation marks and forward slashes to separate lines. If the quoted lines of poetry run more than four lines in your essay, use the format for long quotes above, but take care to retain the original structure of the poem with all unique spacing and line breaks.

## Examples

- Bryant assures his readers that nature speaks "A various language; for his gayer hours / She has a voice of gladness, and a smile / And eloquence of beauty."
- The crumbling statue's "wrinkled lip, and sneer of cold command, / Tell that its sculptor well those passions read."

## Dialogue

Use quotation marks to indicate dialogue. For each new speaker, start a new paragraph and indent 1/2 inch (five spaces).

## Example

"Never marry a woman with straw-colored hair, Dorian," he said, after a few puffs.
"Why, Harry?"
"Because they are so sentimental."
"But I like sentimental people."
"Never marry at all, Dorian. Men marry because they are tired; women, because they are curious. Both are disappointed."
"I don't think I am likely to marry, Harry. I am too much in love. That is one of your aphorisms. I am putting it into practice, as I do everything you say."
**- Oscar Wilde**

## Irony & Invented Terms

Use quotation marks to signal irony and sarcasm Enclose any terms you, as the writer of the essay, have coined or invented.

## Examples

- He said she was "cute."
- The committee "fixed" all of the company's problems. I'll just call it an "axiommaker."
- We should adopt the androgenous pronoun "itt."

# Hyphen

## Compound Adjectives

Use a hyphen to combine multiple words that collectively function as one adjective.

## Examples

- high-minded philosopher
- fast-food restaurant

- thirteen-year-old house
- green-eyed girl
- low-performing district
- cooling-off period
- sea-weed-flavored tofu

**NOTE #1 -** Most compound adjectives come before a noun. Do not hyphenate adjectives that follow a noun.

**Examples**
- Bobby stands six feet tall
- The essay is well written.

**NOTE #2 -** Do not hyphenate adverbs that end in ly.

**Examples**
- fully developed style
- really strong wind
- carefully crafted design

**NOTE #3 -** Do not hyphenate adjectival nouns unless the hyphenation was already present.

**Examples**
- African American culture
- Indo-European roots

**NOTE #4 -** Do not hyphenate compounds that are expressed in one word.

**Examples**
- airfield
- blackboard
- blueprint
- codebreaker
- comeback
- commonsense
- handpicked
- rainforest
- roadblock
- wartime

## Prefixes and Suffixes

Most prefixes and suffixes do not require a hyphen. Notable exceptions include all-, ex-, self-, and -elect (suffix).

### Examples

- all-important factor
- ex-military contractor self-help book
- New York's senator-elect

## Numbers

Hyphenate fractions and numbers below 100.

### Examples

- one-tenth
- three and one-tenth
- fifty-five
- three hundred fifty-five

# Semicolon

## Connect Sentences

Use a semicolon to connect two full sentences. An independent clause (IC) must be present on both sides of the semicolon. Semicolons are most commonly used to connect full sentences that contain closely related ideas. However, semicolons have a bad reputation and should be used sparingly, perhaps only one or two in an entire essay.

## Patterns of Use

IC; IC

IC; ca, IC

### Examples

- I whacked the ball harder than I ever had before; I had hit a home run.
- I whacked the ball harder than I ever had before; however, I had not hit a home run.
- He was not a rich man who was a manufacturer; he was a manufacturer who was incidentally rich.
- Our interest in art is seldom a matter of mere feeling or appreciation; usually, it is a matter of judgment as well.
- Sometimes we took the initiative and started to quell the fire of the Spanish trenches; sometimes they opened upon us.

**NOTE #1 -** Do not use a semicolon before a coordinating conjunction (cc) - and, or, nor, for, but, yet, so.

### Examples

- INCORRECT - I whacked the ball harder than I ever had before; and I had hit a home run.
- INCORRECT - I went to the dentist; but I did not have any cavities.

**NOTE #2 -** Do not use a semicolon between independent and dependent clauses (IC; DC or DC; IC).

### Examples

- INCORRECT - Because I have been experiencing some tooth pain; I went to the dentist today.
- INCORRECT - I went to the dentist today; because I have been experiencing some tooth pain.

### Items in Series Containing Commas

Use semicolons to separate items in a series where commas are already present.

### Examples

- I like guns, ammo, and firecrackers; computers, iPads, and iPhones; good food; and fast cars.
- Men can be aggressive, which is vulgar; short tempered, which is typical; and sometimes even kind, which is just the sort of man seek.

### Legend

**IC** = Independent Clause (full sentence - can stand alone as a complete thought)
**DC** = Dependent Clause (partial sentence - not a complete thought)
**cc** = Coordinating Conjunction (and, or, nor, for, but, yet, so)
**ca** = Conjunctive Adverb (however, moreover, nevertheless, hence, still, etc.)

# Agreement

Make subjects and verbs agree. If the subject of a sentence is singular, then its verb must also be singular. If the subject of a sentence is plural, then its verb must also be plural.

Do not match your verb with any portion of the sentence that is not actually its subject.

### Examples
- A high level of greenhouse gasses causes air pollution. (Do not write "cause" as a match for "gasses.")
- The problem is trust, honesty, and commitment. (Do not write "are" as a match for the series in the predicate. Those three things are functioning as one problem.)

Subjects joined with and are usually treated as plural.

### Example
- Bill and Johnny fish together every Sunday. (Do not write "fishes" as a match for one of the two men.)

Compound subjects that use the words each or every are treated as singular.

### Examples
- Every book, newspaper, and magazine in the library is out of place. (Do not write "are" to match a plural group. You are referring to singular individuals here.)
- Each writer, professor, and critic has a different view on the matter. (Do not write "have" to match a plural group. You are referring to singular individuals here.)

When used as the subject of a sentence, the following words usually require singular verbs -
- Anyone, anybody, anything
- Everyone, everybody, everything
- Somebody, someone, something
- Either, Neither
- No one, Nothing

### Example
- Everyone around here loves the governor. (Do not write "love" thinking that "everyone" is a plural. You are referring to one group.

For compound subjects that use the words *or* or *nor* match the verb with the nearest subject.

> ### Examples
> - A bachelor's degree or several specific courses are required. (Match with "courses.")
> - Several specific courses or a bachelor's degree is required. (Match with "degree.")
> - Neither Billy nor the town elders were able to solve the problem. (Match with "elders.")

# Wrong Word

Be careful not to confuse similar words or mistake the definition of a word and use it improperly. Spell check will not correct wrong word errors.

### affect / effect
Effect is a noun that signifies a result or the ability to produce a result - "Those pills produce negative effects."
Affect is usually a verb that means to influence or change something - "Don't affect me with your negative attitude."

### all right / alright
Alright is incorrect usage. Use all right.

### all together / altogether
All together is used to describe a group - "Please put the scarves all together in one place." * Use All together if you can place other words between *all* and *together* with the sentence still making sense.
Altogether means entirely - "This profession is altogether wrong for me."

### allusion / illusion
Allusion is a noun and denotes a reference to something outside of the current context - "Most of his works of literature contain at least one allusion to mythology."
Illusion is a noun that means something one perceives that is not really there - "The money in that account was just an illusion."

### a lot / alot
Alot is incorrect usage. Use a lot.

### capital / capitol
Capital refers to money, capital letters, and a city where the seat of government is

located - "Austin is the capital of Texas."
Capitol is the building where laws are made - ";We visited the U.S. Capitol last weekend."

## cite / site

Cite is a verb that means to quote or reference something - "Use MLA 2009 to cite your sources."
Cite also means to recognize formally - "I was cited for my philanthropy."
Cite can also mean to summon before a court of law - "When I was eighteen, I was cited for carrying nun-chucks."
Site is a noun that refers to a place - "The site of the crash is blocked off."

## farther / further

Farther is an adjective and adverb for distance - "It is farther from here to New York than I am willing to drive."
Further is an adjective and adverb for degree - "Please explain the problem further."
Further can also be used like the conjunctive adverb moreover - "And I further make it known that I do not concur."

## fewer / less

Fewer is an adjective that is used only when the items can be counted - "I ate fewer pieces of cake."
Less is an adjective that is used with amounts that cannot be counted - "I ate less cake."

## i.e. / e.g.

e.g. means "for example." It comes from the Latin term exempli gratia.
i.e. means "in other words." It comes from the Latin term id est.

## it's / its

It's = It is - "It's a good day to run."
Its = ownership - "Its Adam's baseball."

## laid / lain / lay

Lie means to assume a horizontal resting position (lies, lying, lays, lain)
Lay means to put down (lay, laid).

## principal / principle

Principal is a noun that denotes a position of great authority - "Mr. Smith is the principal of this school."

Principal can also be an adjective similar to the word main - "That is the principal reason I moved to Austin."

Principle is a noun that signifies a guideline or standard - "Our moral principles tell us not to steal."

### their / there / they're
Their shows ownership.

There shows location

They're = they are.

"They're going to be at the rodeo because their horses have a good chance of winning there."

### who's / whose
Who's = who is.

Whose = ownership

"Who's willing to go find out whose car this is?"

### your / you're
Your = ownership.

You're = you are.

"You're the one she wants to race, as long as you don't wear your spikes."

# Titles (Format)

MLA 2009 guidelines require that the titles of various types of works be specifically formatted with either quotation marks or italics. Underlining is no longer used, except in the case of handwritten documents.

### Quotation Marks
Enclose the titles of short works in quotation marks. Ask yourself if the piece is part of a larger work (i.e. part of a whole); if so, enclose its title in quotation marks.

### Types of Works To Write in Quotations
- songs, poems, short stories, essays
- magazine articles, journal articles, book chapters, pages from a website
- works from an anthology

### Examples
- My favorite song is "Stairway to Heaven."
- "The Try-Works" is my favorite chapter of *Moby-Dick*.

- "The Singularity Approaches" is an influential article that appeared in *Time Magazine.*
- *CNN.com* ran a story entitled "Education: Why It Matters."

## Italics

Use italics for works that are NOT parts of a whole -

## Types of Works To Write in Italics

- Books
- Newspapers
- Magazines
- Journals
- Movies
- Albums
- Websites
- Databases

## Examples

- *Moby-Dick* by Herman Melville
- *The New York Times*
- *Journal of the American Medical Association*
- *Forest Gump*
- *Fearless* by Taylor Swift
- *CNN.com*
- *Academic Search Complete*
- *JSTOR*

# Syntax

Syntax is word order. More specifically, syntax is the way an author chooses to group words within clauses, phrases, and sentences. To analyze syntax, look for unique word order and decide how that unique language develops meaning in the text.

## Examples
- "Madness in great ones must not unwatch'd go." vs. Great ones who are mad should not go unwatched. - William Shakespeare
- "Love is not love that alters when it alteration finds." vs. Love is not love that alters when it finds alteration. - William Shakespeare
- "I and this mystery here we stand" vs. This mystery and I stand here - Walt Whitman
- "Here I opened wide the door;" vs. I opened the door wide here - Edgar Allan Poe
- "Whose woods these are I think I know" vs. I think I know whose woods these are. - Robert Frost

## Syntax Techniques

### Juxtaposition
A literary device in which two very dissimilar things (i.e. words, ideas, objects, characters, etc.) are compared or contrasted to achieve a new and interesting effect.

## Examples
- "John Donne - Ann Donne - Undone." - John Donne
- "Were vexed to nightmare by a rocking cradle" - William Butler Yeats
- "No light, but rather darkness rather visible" - John Milton
- "Suddenly I saw the cold and rook-delighting Heaven / That seemed as though ice burned and was but the more ice," - William Butler Yeats

### Omission
The intentional omission of words, clauses, or phrases.

## Examples
- "And he to England shall along with you."- William Shakespeare
- "He works his work, I mine. - Alfred, Lord Tennyson
- "So that, forever rudderless, it went upon the seas / Going ridiculous voyages" - Stephen Crane "The Black Riders"

## Parallel Structure (Parallelism)

Using like grammatical structure, diction, and phrasing to correlate successive clauses and phrases, both within and among sentences.

### Examples

- "Ask not what your country can do for you; ask what you can do for your country." - John F. Kennedy
- "The prince's strength is also his weakness; his self-reliance is also isolation." - Machiavelli
- "There is a time in every man's education when he arrives at the conviction that envy is ignorance; that imitation is suicide; that he must take himself for better, for worse, as his portion;" - Ralph Waldo Emerson

## Repetition

Reusing the same words or phrases for rhythmic or rhetorical effect.

### Example

"We must fight! I repeat it, sir, we must fight!" - Patrick Henry

## Polysyndeton

The use of multiple coordinating conjunctions in series to create a sense of rhythm or a tone of excitement and energy.

### Examples

- "[A]s the wind howled on, and the sea leaped, and the ship groaned and dived, and yet steadfastly shot her red hell further and further into the blackness of the sea and the night, and scornfully champed the white bone in her mouth, and viciously spat round her on all sides; then the rushing Pequod, freighted with savages, and laden with fire, and burning a corpse, and plunging into that blackness of darkness, seemed the material counterpart of her monomaniac commander's soul." - Herman Melville - *Moby-Dick*
- I mete and dole / Unequal laws unto a savage race, / That hoard, and sleep, and feed, and know not me." - Alfred, Lord Tennyson

## Anaphora

The repetition of the same word or group of words at the beginning of neighboring clauses.

### Example

"We shall not flag or fail. We shall go on to the end. We shall fight in France, we shall fight on the seas and oceans, we shall fight with growing confidence and growing strength in the air, we shall defend our island, whatever the cost may be, we shall fight on the beaches, we shall fight on the landing grounds, we shall fight in the fields and in the streets, we shall fight in the hills. We shall never surrender." - Winston Churchill

## Epanalepsis
The repetition at the end of a clause of the word that occurred at the beginning of the clause.

## Examples
- "Possessing what we still were unpossessed by, / Possessed by what we now no more possessed." - Robert Frost
- "To each the boulders that have fallen to each." - Robert Frost
- "The king is dead, long live the king. / What is Hecuba to him, or he to Hecuba?" - William Shakespeare

# Colon

Use a colon to direct attention to a list, an appositive, or a quotation.

**An independent clause (IC) must be present before a colon.**

### Examples
- List - I have so much work to do at home this evening: dishes, yard work, laundry, bills, and vacuuming.
- Appositive - My personality his two serious deficiencies: laziness and gluttony.
- Quotation - This reminds me of what Patrick Henry said: "Give me liberty, or give me death."

**NOTE #1** - Do not use a semicolon before a coordinating conjunction (cc) - and, or, nor, for, but, yet, so.

### Example: Colon Error
- **INCORRECT** - A few important essay-writing skills are: paragraph development, logical analysis, and scholarly research. (No independent clause before the colon.)
- **CORRECT** - A few important essay-writing skills are as follows: paragraph development, logical analysis, and scholarly research.

# Sentences

The type of sentences a writer employs can often have a profound effect on the tone, rhythm, flow, readability, and meaning of his or her essay. Vary the length and type of sentences you use in order to enhance the fluency and flow of your writing and enhance the overall rhetorical effectiveness of your essay.

**Simple Sentence** - A sentence that contains only one independent clause (IC).

### Examples
- I hit the ball.
- The problem is trust and honesty.
- I hit the ball and ran the bases.
- My car skidded out of control.

**Compound Sentence -** A sentence that contains two or more independent clauses joined by a comma and a coordinating conjunction (or by a semicolon).

## Examples
- I hit the ball, and I ran the bases.
- My car skidded out of control, and we hit the guardrail.
- My car skidded out of control, and we hit the guardrail, but that is what saved our lives.

**Complex Sentence -** A sentence that contains one independent clause and one or more dependent clauses (i.e. DC or "subordinate clause").

## Examples
- Because it was the last game of the season, I hit the ball.
- Because it was the last game of the season, I hit the ball as hard as I could.
- Although we still don't know why, my car skidded out of control.
- If you love fishing so much, you should buy a boat. I bought my boat because I love fishing so much.

**Compound-Complex Sentence -** A sentence that contains two or more independent clauses and at least one dependent clause.

## Examples
- Because it was the last game of the season, I hit the ball, and I ran the bases.
- Because it was the last game of the season, I hit the ball as hard as I could, but it was a foul.
- Although we still don't know why, my car skidded out of control, and we hit the guardrail.
- Although we still don't know why, my car skidded out of control, and we hit the guardrail, but that is what saved our lives.
- If you love fishing so much, you should buy a boat, but you shouldn't buy anything you can't afford.
- I bought my boat because
- I love fishing so much, and that was the best decision I ever made.

**Periodic Sentence -** A sentence in which the main idea is not understood until the very end of the sentence. A number of dependent clauses and parallel constructions (i.e. parenthetical elements) lead up to the final independent clause or main thought of the sentence.

**Example**

"Whenever I find myself growing grim about the mouth; whenever it is a damp, drizzly November in my soul; whenever I find myself involuntarily pausing before coffin warehouses, and bringing up the rear of every funeral I meet; and especially whenever my hypos get such an upper hand of me, that it requires a strong moral principle to prevent me from deliberately stepping into the street, and methodically knocking people's hats off -- then, I account it high time to get to sea as soon as I can." - Herman Melville - *Moby-Dick*

**Loose Sentence** - A sentence in which the main idea can be understood from the very beginning. Usually, the main clause of a loose sentence is followed by an extended list of dependent clauses.

**Example**

"I felt an inexpressible relief, a soothing conviction of protection and security, when I knew that there was a stranger in the room, an individual not belonging to Gateshead, and not related to Mrs. Reed." - Charlotte Bronte - *Jane Eyre*

CPSIA information can be obtained at www.ICGtesting.com
Printed in the USA
BVOW05s1046180114

R5605500001B/R56055PG341963BVX9B/16/P